Strategic Alliances Among Health and Human Services Organizations

SAGE SOURCEBOOKS FOR
THE HUMAN SERVICES SERIES

Series Editors: ARMAND LAUFFER and CHARLES GARVIN

Recent Volumes in This Series

Strategic Alliances Among Health and Human Services Organizations

From Affiliations to Consolidations

Sage Sourcebooks for

the Human Services

Darlyne Bailey
Kelly McNally Koney

Sage Publications, Inc.
International Educational and Professional Publisher
Thousand Oaks ■ London ■ New Delhi

For information:

Sage Publications, Inc.
2455 Teller Road
Thousand Oaks, California 91320
E-mail: order@sagepub.com

Sage Publications Ltd.
6 Bonhill Street
London EC2A 4PU
United Kingdom

Sage Publications India Pvt. Ltd.
M-32 Market
Greater Kailash I
New Delhi 110 048 India

Printed in the United States of America

Library of Congress Cataloging-in-Publication Data

Bailey, Darlyne, 1952–
    Strategic alliances among health and human services
organizations: From affiliations to consolidations / by
Darlyne Bailey and Kelly McNally Koney.
        p. cm. —
    (Sage sourcebooks for the human services series ; v. 41)
    Includes bibliographical references and index.
    ISBN 0-7619-1315-7 (cloth: alk. paper)
    ISBN 0-7619-1316-5 (pbk.: alk. paper)
    1. Strategic alliances (Business) 2. Interorganizational relations.
    I. Koney, Kelly McNally. II. Title. III. Series.
    HD69.S8 B347 2000
    658'.044—dc21   99-050898

This book is printed on acid-free paper.

00 01 02 03 04 05 06 7 6 5 4 3 2 1

Acquisition Editor:	Nancy Hale
Editorial Assistant:	Heidi van Middlesworth
Production Editor:	Sanford Robinson
Editorial Assistant:	Cindy Bear
Typesetter:	Tina Hill
Indexer:	Molly Hall
Cover Designer:	Candice Harman

CONTENTS

PREFACE

Today, many nonprofit health and human service organizations (HSOs) are engaging in discussions about the formation of coalitions, mergers, and other types of interorganizational alliances. Interorganizational alliances among HSOs are not really new. They have been documented clearly throughout the 20th century and may actually date back to the formation of some of the first organizations. But present-day alliances are emerging in a very different sociopolitical context, with significant financial, programmatic, and, ultimately, structural consequences for HSOs as well as for the broader nonprofit sector.

Indeed, the nonprofit environment in which most HSOs operate is so laden with multiple and interrelated challenges that it is considered by some to be in "an emerging crisis" (Salamon, 1997, p. 11). These challenges include the growing competition for control of programs and funding from other nonprofit as well as for-profit organizations, declining financial support from traditional funders, and heightened community need. Faced with such issues and the new realities of managed care and welfare reform, HSOs are feeling powerful internal and external pressures to diversify, redesign, and expand their programs and services at the same time that they are being asked by their boards, funders, and other stakeholders to increase efficiency, effectiveness, and accountability.

How can an HSO caught in such a dilemma successfully respond to all of these issues? The answer, as many are discovering, is by partnering with other organizations, pooling their resources, and using their newly combined strength to leverage additional resources in the furtherance of their common goals.

All of this activity has led to an exciting, yet anxiety-filled future for HSOs as organizational transformation is becoming almost an imperative. Even as second- and third-generation welfare reform issues remain focused on reducing caseloads, and managed care changes the nature of medical, mental health, and child welfare service delivery, evidence of the need for health and human services is mounting. Thus, HSOs are faced with negotiating a balance between responding to community needs and their own need for organizational survival.

At the same time, growing numbers of these organizations are discovering that joining forces with other organizations can enable them to extend the impact of their resources and expertise beyond current organizational or community boundaries. Following a trend that has occurred among for-profit organizations and is now being seen throughout the nonprofit sector, public and private HSOs are aligning their efforts to ensure broader service presence across cities, counties, and even states. They are creating partnerships to build greater capacity and working together to create community-driven initiatives.

The potential of such alliances to have a positive impact on individuals, agencies, and the nonprofit sector overall cannot be underestimated. Some of these interorganizational responses focus on sharing programs or shaping policy, others on education, research, or other goals, but the result is that both large and small HSOs are joining forces and learning from and with each other. And, with HSOs facing increasingly complex demands in the form of legislative reform, continued movement toward more community-based and integrated services, and mandates for greater accountability, the trend toward interorganizational activity seems likely to continue.

Many insights into these activities have been captured by the growing literature on federated organizing, coalition building, service integration, and strategic restructuring. This book, which is intended to complement that body of work, is an attempt to pull this material together and create a coherent framework for thinking about strategic alliances—along with a set of practical tools for building and maintaining them—that frontline practitioners and students of the nonprofit sector can use to come to terms with the pressures facing HSOs today.

This book begins with the premise that simply asking HSOs to work harder is not an adequate response to the present challenges; nor will this strategy by itself succeed in appropriately positioning these organizations for the future. HSOs, regardless of size, must continue to push out their boundaries. The administrators of HSOs and other nonprofit organizations, their boards of trustees and staffs, and community leaders must be willing and able to form appropriate alliances with other organizations—including those with seemingly divergent goals—for the advancement of common tasks and the realization of shared missions. This book is intended to serve as a guide in that process.

OUR APPROACH

This book, in short, is about the development and maintenance of strategic alliances. For students and organizations new to this type of work, we first explore the formation of strategic alliances both in theory and in practice. We describe the preconditions and motives that lead organizations to form interorganizational alliances and provide examples of how they do so. For practitioners, board members, and agencies already involved in creating such partnerships, we believe that this book offers much helpful information, along with practical tips on how to sustain, recreate, and, where necessary, end these partnerships. The dynamic character and key aspects of the strategic alliance maintenance process are illustrated with real-life organizational experiences gleaned from more than a decade of work with local and national strategic alliances.

Information provided here includes material collected through evaluation and consultation with strategic alliances large and small. It also includes illustrative findings from a recent research project conducted in partnership with a second team of researchers at the Mandel Center for Nonprofit Organizations at Case Western Reserve University in Cleveland, Ohio, which has been studying strategic alliances as well. We jointly conducted a national survey exploring the experiences of 75 organizations that participated in strategic alliances. Data from this research have been incorporated throughout this book, and the cases contained in these chapters were generated in connection with this study.

Beyond offering theoretical frameworks and practical applications for understanding how strategic alliances are created and sustained, we hope to clarify some of the confusion surrounding terminology that often occurs when people talk about these interorganizational relationships. While the practice of building strategic alliances is becoming increasingly common, the consistent and uniform usage of relevant terms is not. In fact, with the growth in formation of strategic alliances, the vocabulary used to discuss these partnerships is becoming, if anything, more confusing. For example, what is the difference between coordination and collaboration? Is the neighborhood council an affiliation, a coalition, or a consortium? And what do these terms mean, anyway?

This book begins to answer these and other questions by establishing a theoretical foundation and a conceptual framework for describing these various options with the goal of assisting individuals and organizations as they conceptualize, create, and sustain strategic alliances. It focuses primarily on the development of alliances among HSOs in urban and suburban communities, but it offers this material in a form that is also relevant to HSOs based in rural areas. Similarly, because the subjects of the case applications discussed here are largely private, nonprofit organizations, the strategic alliances under examination are predominantly private-private partnerships. However, feedback gathered during the long process of refining this material through presentations and practice suggests that the material is also germane to the experiences of public-public and public-private partnerships.

This book examines 10 strategic alliance models that are representative of the partnerships currently being formed by HSOs. We have tried to show where each of these models fits within a larger theoretical framework, and we have identified key concepts and critical issues associated with the establishment and evolution of each. Finally, the book concludes with the examination of one methodology for evaluating these alliances.

THE GOALS AND
ORGANIZATION OF THIS BOOK

This book is, fundamentally, about relationship building. Strategic alliances involve organizational relationships at many levels and, ultimately, rely on the individual and community relationships underlying their very existence and ability to function. With this in mind, we have set out to do five things:

1. Present the major theoretical frameworks associated with the formation and maintenance of interorganizational relationships
2. Describe a conceptual framework for the development of these relationships over time

3. Discuss the continuum of strategic alliances, highlighting specific models that range from loosely connected affiliations to statutorily defined mergers and consolidations

4. Offer practical examples that apply these conceptual data to the leadership and development of these interorganizational forms

5. Suggest one framework for evaluating the effectiveness and accountability of these alliances

We have sought to achieve these goals by using a combination of different but complementary approaches. First, we present the conceptual framework that forms the basis for understanding what is involved in alliances in general and in each particular type of alliance. Then, we illustrate these concepts with practical applications drawn from the real world of HSOs. You, the reader, must determine how well these goals have been met.

This book is arranged by six topical areas. Part I lays the foundation by discussing the central concepts underlying the formation and development of strategic alliances. Thus, the three chapters in Part I describe the language, theoretical perspectives, fundamental components, developmental stages, and legal considerations of strategic alliances. Parts II through V focus on the four general classifications into which all strategic alliances can be grouped: cooperation, coordination, collaboration, and what we have termed *coadunation*. In these processes, the relationships among the organizational partners become progressively more integrated and formal.

These classifications provide the organizing framework for the remainder of the book. Chapters 4 through 10 in Parts II through V explore 10 models for structuring strategic alliances that fall under these general classifications. Each chapter provides a description of the model followed by a case summary and a more comprehensive case study illustrating its application. Each chapter concludes with reflections from the case reporter and a preliminary analysis of the case that highlights some of its critical elements.

Part VI completes the book with a discussion of how such information can be used to evaluate the effectiveness of strategic alliances as well as to strengthen the alliance's own process. Once again, a case summary drawn from actual HSO experiences is used to show how the components described earlier in the book figure in the development and evaluation of an alliance, and how an ongoing evaluation process known as participatory action research enabled the organizations involved to resolve issues as they arose. A short afterword concludes this book, remembering earlier work in this area of strategic alliances; acknowledging our present level of understanding; and welcoming future alliance research, education, and practice.

Despite the fact that we discuss relevant conceptual frameworks and recommend appropriate tools and concepts for developing strategic alliances, this book should not be taken as a blueprint for engaging in this process. The theories, frameworks, and models around which this book is structured are just that: *ideal* types that offer readers ways to organize their understanding of alliances. They provide guides and benchmarks, and they outline broad, but not exhaustive, categories and components to consider in the development, maintenance, and, where appropriate, termination of alliances.

In sum, this book combines classic and cutting-edge theoretical and practice-based information from the health and human service domains to illustrate the process and content issues involved in the establishment and maintenance of the various forms of nonprofit alliances. Both case studies and other material based on actual strategic alliance experiences are used to illustrate core elements of the frameworks in order to better inform the decisions made by individuals and organizations regarding their leadership of and participation in these interorganizational alliances. Understanding these critical components, their relationships, and some of the legal issues involved, organizational representatives in strategic alliances will be better equipped to work effectively with these interorganizational forms.

There is one other salient feature of this book that should be noted. In contrast to other publications in this area, this book focuses deliberately on a broad spectrum of strategic alliances that are seen frequently among HSOs. The reason for this focus is that, just as there are features that differentiate alliance models from one another, there are characteristics of nonprofit alliances that distinguish them from for-profit partnerships. Grounding relevant frameworks in the experiences of HSOs participating in a variety of alliance models provides useful information to other HSOs as they consider or engage in similar efforts.

Although there is still much to be learned from the lessons of our for-profit counterparts, HSOs considering or already participating in alliances have much to teach and learn from others regardless of the structure of their particular alliance. We believe that this book advances our understanding of this teaching/learning process and thus better informs the thoughts and actions of organizations from all sectors that find themselves engaged in the challenges of creating and maintaining strategic alliances. We welcome you, our readers, as partners on this journey!

ACKNOWLEDGMENTS

Together, we are grateful to many people for their continued support and interest in our work and this book. Specifically, we want to thank the students in our interorganizational relations courses. In the process of teaching, we learned so much about strategic alliances from them. We would like to thank our colleagues at the Mandel School of Applied Social Sciences at Case Western Reserve University, including David Campbell, John Yankey, and the Strategic Alliance Project Team at the Mandel Center for Nonprofit Organizations. They listened, read drafts of the book, and were partners with us in research.

We want to recognize the special efforts of Nina Aronoff, Fumi Sakamoto, Sharon Gamble, Susan Freimark, and Dennis Dooley, who helped us clarify and refine our thoughts. We also want to acknowledge Laura Chisolm at the Case Western Reserve University School of Law for her valuable input on the legal aspects of strategic alliances discussed throughout this book.

Additionally, we appreciate the work of Fran Danis and all of the organizational reporters featured herein. They wholeheartedly shared their experiences with us, and through their stories, this book is richer and so are we. Similarly, the "partners in real world" alliances we have met through our work have offered us invaluable resources. The questions they asked us and the encouragement they provided throughout this process convinced us that this book was needed to help fill a gap within and between the worlds of scholarship and practice.

We also want to extend a special thanks to Jim Nageotte, Nancy Hale, and Heidi van Middlesworth at Sage Publications. They provided us with continuous support and technical assistance throughout this project.

Finally, we want to express our unending appreciation to our families. They have believed in each of us and in us together as a dynamic alliance that has existed for close to a decade. Their continuous love and support have helped to sustain and uplift this journey.

Part I

WHEN ORGANIZATIONS COME TOGETHER

The Fundamentals of Strategic Alliances

In response to growing competition for scarce resources and other pressures, rising numbers of organizations are learning that by partnering with others, they can better position themselves to realize their goals and objectives. The formation of such interorganizational partnerships, or strategic alliances, is occurring not only in the for-profit sector, but also increasingly in the nonprofit sector. The seeming paradox is that health and human service organizations (HSOs), which once saw one another as rivals, suddenly find themselves thinking about working together.

Unfortunately, alliances do not always work out the way the partners expect; even in the more successful ones, tensions can develop, draining staff and board time and energies. Ultimately, these challenges may threaten alliance cohesiveness and decrease the chances that the organizations can achieve their desired results. These situations happen frequently because of a basic underlying issue: As the process begins, the partner organizations are not sufficiently clear with one another, or with themselves, about what they mean by a strategic alliance. Indeed, many well-meaning organizations rush into these relationships without having seriously considered what it is going to take to realize or sustain them.

With this in mind, this section of the book aims to build a common understanding between the prospective partners and give them the practical tools they will need to build a successful alliance. Chapter 1 explores the key concepts that underlie all strategic alliances and provides language to use in talking about them. Chapter 2 looks at six prime movers for organizations seeking alliances and how these motivators shape the expectations that organizations bring to the process. Chapter 3 examines the critical components of an alliance and the natural lifecycle through which every alliance evolves.

Although strategic alliances may take different forms and develop along different paths, all share certain features. Armed with a deeper understanding of these fundamentals, organizations contemplating an alliance will be better able to make an informed decision about whether, and what kind of alliance, to join and will be more prepared to plan for its long-term success. The leaders and members of existing alliances may discover the sources of obstacles while simultaneously uncovering hidden strengths and ways in which these strengths can be mobilized to better realize the goals of the alliance.

Chapter 1

WHAT ARE STRATEGIC ALLIANCES?

Thinking broadly, one can say that people have always been forming strategic alliances. In personal relationships, they partner with each other hoping to realize their own and their mutual goals. Similarly, people are members of book clubs, investment groups, and neighborhood watches to achieve synergies associated with collective rather than individual action. Even institutions such as banks and school districts function as alliances because they enable individuals and organizations to do more together than most could do on their own. They accomplish these things by pooling resources, sharing risks, and dividing costs and benefits.

In recent years, growing numbers of health and human service organizations (HSOs) have been entering into strategic alliances with each other for reasons not all that different from those just mentioned. Yet relative to the frequency with which these relationships are being formed, little time has been spent in trying to understand what strategic alliances involve and how they can be most productive.

So, what, then, are strategic alliances? To put it in the simplest terms, strategic alliances are multiparty relationships, and regardless of whether these partnerships occur among individuals or organizations, each such alliance is defined by two distinct elements: its strategy and the form of its relationship. The former has to do with what each party is hoping to accomplish by entering into the relationship and how the parties intend to achieve their goals. The latter has to do with the way in which the relationship will be created and maintained: who will be responsible for what, how decisions will be made, how resources will be allocated, who will be accountable to whom, what areas of activity will be shared or combined, and in what areas, if any, autonomy will be retained.

More specifically, the term *alliance* describes a macrolevel relationship between two or more entities with a similar interest that implies a willingness to engage in ongoing relationship-building. Both the obligations and the outcomes of the alliance are shared. Alliances are *strategic* when they are formed for an expressed purpose or purposes. Because of the mission-driven emphasis of the nonprofit sector, there must be a connection between this purpose and the implementation of the organization's mission. Therefore, in this book, strategic alliances are defined as *intentional, interorganizational relationships created to benefit the organizational partners and, ultimately, the organizations' consumers.*

It is important to note that the term *strategic alliance* does not define the *process* of working together, nor, as it is used in this book, is it considered a specific *type* of interorganizational relationship. It is an umbrella concept that includes various processes and under which multiple models of interorganizational relationships can occur. This distinction between process and model, or type, is an important one in creating and maintaining strategic alliances. This chapter begins to clarify this distinction, and Parts II through V of this book further demonstrate the relationship between these concepts.

A WORD ABOUT TERMINOLOGY

Just as there are many possible strategies that an organization might adopt in creating strategic alliances, so there are different types of alliances possible. Therefore, it is important at the outset to be clear about which kind of partnership one is talking about—indeed, which options present themselves, with what advantages and disadvantages, and what would make one more appropriate for a particular situation than for another.

Defining exactly what kind of strategic alliance people or organizations are talking about can be difficult, and much of what has been written on the subject only makes matters more complicated. The problem is largely one of vocabulary.

Some of the language used to describe strategic alliances has been established by statutes; some has been generated through practical usage. However, many of the terms associated with interorganizational relations in the literature, in practice, and in classrooms are often used indiscriminately and in ways that can be contradictory. To make matters worse, the same terms are not necessarily used the same way in the legal arena as they are in organizational settings, making them appear even more ambiguous and, in many cases, simply confusing. This inconsistency is, in part, the result of the fact that much of the initial practice on which this vocabulary was based involved for-profit organizations and international political parties, and the terms are not wholly transferable. Moreover, as times have changed, the use of various terms has changed as well.

Another common problem in the way strategic alliances are discussed is the tendency not to make a clear distinction between the process of working together and the form or structure that such interorganizational activity takes (Kagan, 1991). This kind of confusion is often found, for example, in funding guidelines that call for the creation of collaborations but mean the formation of some type of strategic alliance such as a coalition or a consortium. Similarly, grant applicants frequently are mandated to create partnerships but are left to determine the specifics of the strategic alliance process and structure on their own. Without consistency in language, this task is considerably more difficult, and creative interpretation only exacerbates the use of divergent terminology.

Finally, when alliances are named, members often give less consideration to accurately describing the type of the alliance than to the marketability of the name. In several of the cases presented later in this book, the alliances chose their names based largely on how they sounded to the members. In one case, the alliance began with "consortium," but after it was formed, the alliance was renamed a coalition. In fact, the term coalition more accurately described the structure and purpose of the alliance, but these were not significant factors in its selection. The alliance changed its name because the members felt it sounded better.

WHY USING UNIFORM LANGUAGE IS IMPORTANT

Some might minimize the language issue by arguing that interorganizational alliances are continuing to develop in spite of these incongruities. Yet there is a case to be made for consistency. Using uniform language to talk about things limits the opportunity for misunderstandings. Common terminology enables organizations that are discussing or forming strategic alliances to engage in more precise conversation and to have a clearer mutual understanding of what it is their participation means. It also ensures greater accountability both within the alliance and to external stakeholders.

When an organization is exploring participation in an alliance, it is essential that the organization understand clearly what impact this new relationship will have on it in such areas as autonomy and allocation of, or access to, resources. Using consistent terminology to describe the processes and structures of joint activity increases the likelihood that the participating parties will reach a satisfactory understanding in such matters.

Moreover, shared language facilitates comparison between and among alliances. HSO alliances have much to share with, and learn from, other alliances within and outside their issue areas. When they are trying to learn from each other's experiences, relevant comparisons are essential. Measuring one alliance's experiences against another's does not generate useful data unless the similarities and differences of the models are understood as well. The use of uniform language supports this practice and better informs those trying to learn from it.

A WHOLE RANGE OF POSSIBLE RELATIONSHIPS

One challenge in comparing strategic alliance experiences is the inconsistent use of the terms *cooperation, coordination,* and *collaboration.* Much of the literature on strategic alliances among HSOs distinguishes among these three terms, placing them in a hierarchy or progression (Kagan, 1991; Mattessich & Monsey, 1992; Winer & Ray, 1994). Peterson (1991) suggests that the processes inherent in creating and sustaining strategic alliances form a continuum of interactions. This continuum moves from cooperation to coordination to collaboration:

- In *cooperation,* fully autonomous entities share information to support each other's organizational activities.
- In *coordination,* otherwise autonomous groups align activities, sponsor particular events, or deliver targeted services in pursuit of compatible goals.
- In *collaboration,* parties work collectively through common strategies. Each relinquishes some degree of autonomy toward the realization of a jointly determined purpose.

Cooperation, coordination, and collaboration describe the processes that take place as strategic alliances function. The terms clarify the extent to which members work together to achieve their goals and describe much of the interorganizational activity occurring among HSOs. However, con-

Shared Information & Mutual Support	Common Tasks & Compatible Goals	Integrated Strategies & Collective Purpose	Unified Structure & Combined Cultures

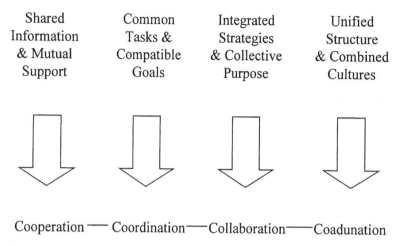

Cooperation ⎯ Coordination⎯Collaboration⎯Coadunation

Figure 1.1. Defining Strategic Alliance Processes

sidering the full range of strategic alliance models that is being formed, it is clear that the continuum is not complete. A fourth interorganizational process exists and is becoming increasingly common among HSOs. It is called *coadunation:*

- In *coadunation,* member organizations unite within an integrated structure to the extent that one or all relinquish their autonomy in favor of a surviving organization.

Coadunation completes the four-level continuum of interorganizational alliance processes (see Figure 1.1). Each of these four processes is further detailed and illustrated in Chapters 4 through 10.

HOW CONNECTED DO YOU WANT TO BE?

While the continuum of interorganizational alliance processes moves from cooperation to coadunation, it also moves from a low degree to a high degree of organizational integration. In other words, members in coadunated alliances are more interdependent as they seek to achieve their goals than are members in collaborative, coordinated, or cooperative alliances.

As organizational integration, or interdependence, increases along the continuum, the need for formalization also increases. Formalization is defined as the extent to which interactions among members are governed by policies and procedures, contracts, and laws (Hage & Aiken, 1967; Van de Ven & Ferry, 1980). As organizational members become more interdependent, they experience a greater need for formalization to establish the parameters of their relationship. Thus, the more thoroughly integrated the member organizations are, the more formally defined is the relationship. Conversely, members in more formal alliances have a greater capability to effect change in each other's organizational policies, procedures, and, consequently, organizational activities, thus making them more integrated.

With the advantage of integration to achieve more complex goals than organizations could address on their own, there is also a potential disadvantage. The degree to which organizational activities are integrated reduces the autonomy each organization has to make its own decisions and increases the risks to each member for its participation in the alliance. As such, the organizational members in less formal alliances have more autonomy and assume less risk than do members in more formal alliances. This means that in moving along the process continuum from cooperation to coadunation, the alliance has more authority to prescribe member behavior, thus requiring a greater investment from member organizations, and the goals and activities of member organizations are more interconnected (see Figure 1.2).

However, these are only some of the features of interorganizational alliances that vary along the strategic alliance continuum. Structural complexity, or the extent to which the alliance is composed of multiple, interrelated parts (Alter, 1990; Lawrence & Lorsch, 1969; Van de Ven & Ferry, 1980), and other features such as governance and resource dependence also become more integrated or increase as the strategic alliance process becomes more formal and interdependent. These, along with other characteristics of the four strategic alliance processes, are discussed in more detail in Parts II through V of this book.

CHOOSING AMONG ALLIANCE MODELS
AND DEGREES OF CONNECTION

Along the continuum of strategic relationships, there are many alliance models among which HSOs can choose. This book describes 10 that

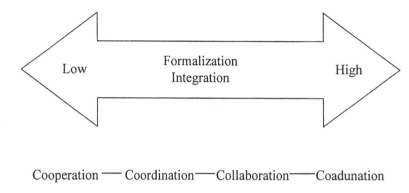

Figure 1.2. Strategic Alliance Processes Along a Continuum

occur frequently in the nonprofit sector: affiliations, federations, associations, coalitions, consortia, networks, joint ventures, mergers, consolidations, and acquisitions. These models do not represent an exhaustive list of the various ways in which nonprofit organizations can work together. There are numerous variations on these. However, the models discussed here are representative of the possibilities, varying in level of organizational integration and formalization. They offer a foundation from which to construct a more comprehensive understanding of the range of models from which HSOs can select in creating strategic alliances.

Each of these 10 alliance models can be classified according to its central process on the continuum of strategic alliances. Its position on the continuum provides clues as to the structure and systems of the alliance, that is, its degree of formalization, as well as the interdependence among members, or integration. For that reason, one of the central themes around which this book is organized is that an alliance of HSOs collaborating toward a specific goal, as in the consortium, network, or joint venture models, is different from an alliance that is based on cooperation, as in the affiliation model. Following similar logic, these processes and alliances differ from alliances that coordinate their activities, as seen in the association, federation, or coalition models, or in alliances that form official unions, as in the case of merger, consolidation, and acquisition models (see Figure 1.3). Furthermore, recognizing these differences is critical to the development and overall success of these alliances.

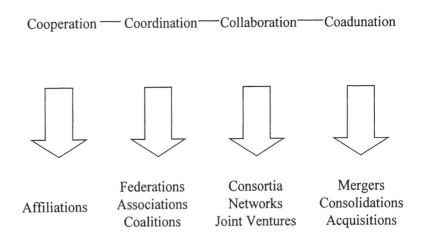

Figure 1.3. Relating Strategic Alliance Processes and Models

THE FINE ART OF BUILDING A RELATIONSHIP

Building a truly effective alliance also depends on how well the prospective partners understand and handle several core aspects of the relationship. Gray and Wood (1991) identify three broad areas of alliance development: correctly assessing the *preconditions* for forming an alliance, successfully negotiating the *process,* and thinking through the desired *outcomes.*

So, how do you know whether a strategic alliance is warranted or would be helpful, or even whether such an arrangement is practical? One answer lies in recognizing and acknowledging the preconditions driving the development or maintenance of the alliance. *Preconditions* are those factors or circumstances that make strategic alliances possible. They are also the motivators that make an organization's participation in an alliance desirable. From a macro perspective, preconditions for strategic alliances can be defined as any conditions affecting the larger environment in which the organization must function; from a micro perspective, they are factors within an individual organization that have made an alliance important. Examples include the threat of competition from a larger entity offering similar services to the organization's consumers (macro level); a transition in leadership and, therefore, leadership style (micro level); or the potential loss of a significant funding source (macro level and micro level).

Once the motivating factors supporting the alliance have been duly considered and discussed, and the prospect of an alliance deemed appropriate, the organizations involved must turn their attention to the process. The alliance *process,* simply put, is the way in which the new partnership is developed and sustained. Indeed, because any complex arrangement must be realized in stages, it describes the course through which the alliance evolves.

The success of any strategic alliance process is dependent on the input of eight closely linked components—leadership, membership, environmental linkages, purpose, strategies, structure, systems, and tasks—and proceeds through a series of predictable phases. (The phases and components of strategic alliance development are discussed in Chapter 3.) The synergy achieved by these components is critical to the success of the alliance process.

The adoption of a specific strategic alliance model is integral to the alliance process. Likewise, the way a particular model allows the resulting alliance to be evaluated, through the systematic collection of information for measurement and improvement, must also be part of the process. It is the way the alliance components are organized that defines the alliance model and provides the baseline data for the ongoing evaluation of the model's effectiveness as well as the overall effectiveness of the process itself. Moreover, there is a basic relationship between the components and the phases that, when attended to, can significantly affect the evolution of the alliance. (Subsequent chapters of this book explore the defining characteristics of each model within the strategic alliance continuum, and a more detailed discussion of the evaluation of strategic alliances will be found in Chapter 11.)

The success of a strategic alliance, in the end, is judged by its outcomes. These may include everything from specific services or products to the results of its activities as perceived by the community. In other words, *outcomes* are any measurable attainments in the furtherance of the alliance's goals. They consist of external achievements—such as the impact of service delivery (e.g., achieving a regional presence and the proportional increase in services provided)—and they consist of successes tied directly to the strategic alliance process itself—such as developing a common mission and goals. The outcomes of the strategic alliance are anything that illustrates its accomplishments and provides a basis for determining whether it fulfilled its purpose.

THE BENEFITS OF WORKING TOGETHER

The decision whether to participate in a strategic alliance requires one other important piece of self-analysis on the part of an HSO, regardless of whether the HSO is pursuing the formation of an alliance or was approached to be a member of one. To make an informed choice, an organizational cost-benefit analysis must first be done. In other words, the HSO must ask itself candidly whether the advantages of participating in the alliance outweigh the disadvantages. This may not be an easy decision for an HSO to make, in part because the benefits of alliance membership may accrue over the long term, whereas the costs may be more evident in the short term. Nevertheless, this assessment of costs and benefits is an essential preliminary step in successful alliance formation and in the ultimate evaluation of the alliance.

Existing research from the nonprofit sector provides some useful insights into the perceived advantages and disadvantages of forming alliances. Although the specific opportunities and obstacles of alliance participation are as individual as each prospective alliance and its members, the following discussion provides an overview of the vast array of benefits that can accrue to alliance participants.

For one thing, strategic alliances offer members the benefit of enhancing their resource base. Membership in a strategic alliance has enabled member organizations to improve their physical facilities and technological systems; increase information sharing; and tap into a larger pool of human resources, providing them with greater capacity and expertise (Croan & Lees, 1979; Kohm, 1998; O'Looney, 1994; Zlotnick, n.d.). Strategic alliances can also serve as an effective vehicle for accessing more or different funding sources, while enabling member organizations to allocate funds and other resources more equitably and use these resources more effectively (Beatrice, 1990; Kohm, 1998; O'Brien & Collier, 1991).

An alliance offers members a forum through which they can have greater input into the management of broader issues that may be beyond their individual scope or capabilities (Black, 1983; Cohen, Baer, & Satterwhite, n.d.). In the same way, an alliance can mobilize the resources of multiple organizations and constituencies to address a pressing community issue, as well as provide safety in numbers when the issue is controversial or threatening to stakeholders (Beatrice, 1990; Rosenthal & Mizrahi, 1994; Salzburg Seminar Core Session 341, Non-Governmental Organizations, group discussion, October 5-12, 1996).

Alliances foster relationships among organizations that may not ordi-
narily work together and thus stimulate new ideas for service delivery and
organizational change. They encourage creativity and innovation in how
organizations conceptualize issues and the ways to manage them and support consensus building among members (Black, 1983; Kagan, 1991).
Such partnerships can also increase organizational visibility within and
outside the issue domain.

Besides improving the quality of, and access to, services, multiorgani-
zational alliances tend to promote organizational and systems reforms
(Kagan, 1991; O'Brien, 1996; Rosenthal & Mizrahi, 1994). They offer
the possibility of co-locating services to provide one-stop shopping for
consumers and expand the practical effectiveness of referral linkages
among agencies, as well as increasing communication (O'Looney, 1994;
Parsons, Jorgensen, & Hernandez, 1994).

Strategic partnerships also offer the benefit of allocating responsibilities for specific tasks to the organizations or groups most equipped to perform them. Such delegation of work can save time (e.g., in planning or
training) and increase employee productivity. Likewise, smart alliances
can result in more efficient information gathering, dissemination, and
service delivery (La Piana, 1997; O'Looney, 1994).

Finally, strategic alliances offer the potential for larger scale impact in
service delivery and public policy or legislative reform (Fisher & Karger,
1997; Haynes & Mickelson, 1997; Salzburg Seminar Core Session 341,
Non-Governmental Organizations, group discussion, October 5-12,
1996). They provide a forum to affect the distribution of power among organizations and give single organizations more power in a particular issue
domain than it could have amassed alone (Black, 1983; Kagan, 1991;
Rosenthal & Mizrahi, 1994).

SOME CAUTIONS BEFORE YOU PROCEED

Although strategic alliances provide numerous opportunities for organizational members and consumers, they are not without their obstacles.
Alliance membership can entail the real or perceived diversion of tangi-
ble and intangible organizational resources in support of the partnership
itself. These resources can include funding, time, identity, autonomy,
flexibility, values or priorities, services, information, and ideas
(Beatrice, 1990; Black, 1983; Croan & Lees, 1979; Kagan, 1991; La
Piana, 1993; Salzburg Seminar Core Session 341, Non-Governmental

Organizations, group discussion, October 5-12, 1996; Zlotnik, n.d.). The new emphasis on inclusion and consensus building that comes with the partnering of HSOs often results in a more time-consuming process than it does in a single organization. The need to negotiate multiple organizational hierarchies also can delay activities. The commitment of time and other resources to the alliance by organizational representatives may be more than the organization prefers or can afford. In addition, organizations considering strategic alliances may be hesitant to relinquish any of their autonomy or may worry that potential compromises will conflict with their organizational values.

In assessing alliance costs and benefits, it is important to remember that these features of alliance membership are not static. They can change as the alliance changes. For this reason, evaluating the benefits of organizational participation in an alliance in relationship to its costs must be an ongoing process. Furthermore, it is a process that needs to be undertaken both by member organizations individually and by the alliance as a whole. In this way, the alliance can adjust to threats to its survival, and it can identify strengths and successes on which it can continue to build.

Chapter 2

SIX ORGANIZING FRAMEWORKS

Just as people enter into personal relationships for a variety of reasons, so, too, do organizations seek strategic alliances in response to certain perceived needs. Indeed, there are many very real advantages to entering into such partnerships. But, as with entering a personal relationship, it is important to go into an alliance with all parties having a clear understanding of one another's needs and expectations with regard to the new partnership.

By better understanding what each HSO is seeking to achieve in the alliance, members of the alliance (including leaders) will be better able to develop goals and objectives that address the various desires of all involved. This does not mean just clearly defining the overall purpose of the alliance; rather, it means exploring what underlying motivators bring the member organizations to the alliance and are likely to keep them participating.

Understanding why organizations are joining an alliance provides an ongoing context for understanding members' input and feedback, as well as offering clues for how to best approach them when soliciting their support. Gathering such information early in the process can help leaders and members structure the alliance to best meet the often compatible, and sometimes seemingly contradictory, needs that evolve. It can provide a valuable theoretical perspective or organizing framework through which leaders can make sense of alliance developments and the conflicts that can occur among alliance members. A clear, organizing framework is helpful in building a strong alliance and in negotiating satisfactory resolutions to those conflicts that naturally occur. Using a variety of case summaries, this chapter looks more closely at six different conceptual frameworks for forming or entering into a strategic alliance.

WHY ORGANIZATIONS SEEK PARTNERSHIPS

Regardless of whether HSOs elect to cooperate, coordinate, collaborate, or coadunate, the fact is that the choice to work together involves many considerations on multiple levels. Although some authors see economics, the concern for survival, the desire for greater efficiency, or the desire for power as typical driving forces behind alliances, the precipitating factors may just as likely be based on external conditions as they are on internal operational goals (Bailey & Koney, 1996; McLaughlin, 1998; Oliver, 1990; Singer & Yankey, 1991; Wernet & Jones, 1992; Yankey, Wester, & Campbell, 1998). Furthermore, motivations for strategic alliance participation may even involve some combination of these. In sum, reasons for forming strategic alliances are as individual as the organizations that engage in them.

Indeed, this has always been the case. Throughout history, environmental trends and external pressures have led to the development of strategic alliances among HSOs. In the early 1900s, growing donor concerns about the uncoordinated state of community planning and fund-raising for health and social welfare organizations led to the federated fund-raising movement in the United States (Cutlip, 1965). Local groups of community organizations formed federations, which later became Community Chests or United Ways, to centralize these activities. The broad-based needs of urban centers following World War II prompted the creation of public-private partnerships aimed at community and economic development (Koebel, Steinberg, & Dyck, 1998). Today, in response to the more recent movement toward managed care, HSOs are creating networks of service providers that often operate as management service organizations (Arsenault, 1998; Emenhiser, King, Joffe, & Penkert, 1998).

Internal and mission-driven goals have also prompted the development of strategic alliances over time. In the 1960s, efforts to coordinate the provision of clinical and nonclinical mental health services for clients resulted in community-based partnerships (Boone & Mannino, 1965). Similar trends toward alliance building to enhance service delivery continued throughout the 1980s. During this time, coalitions to strengthen advocacy efforts for specific client populations and to increase access to resources became prevalent interorganizational forms that continue to be built to effect change today (Croan & Lees, 1979; Fisher & Karger, 1997; Haynes & Mickelson, 1997; Roberts-DeGennaro, 1986, 1987).

Although there is historical precedent for the establishment of interorganizational alliances among HSOs, attention to such alliances in the literature is often overshadowed by research on the formation of alliances in the for-profit sector. One early review of the literature classified the research in the area of interorganizational relations according to four orientations: public administration, marketing, economic, and sociological (Whetten, 1981).

The studies grounded in the public administration and sociological approaches included research on public and nonprofit alliances. However, the experiences of nonprofit organizations generally were absent from the research emerging from the marketing and economic traditions (Whetten, 1981). Similarly, until recently, the theoretical basis for understanding the motivators for organizational partnerships relied more on the experiences of for-profit organizations than on those of their nonprofit counterparts.

A THEORETICAL FRAMEWORK FOR UNDERSTANDING STRATEGIC ALLIANCE MOTIVATORS

The literature on interorganizational relations includes several studies that examine the theoretical frameworks explaining the development of strategic alliances (Gray & Wood, 1991; Oliver, 1990; Reitan, 1998). Overall, these studies have come up with somewhat different, yet complementary, explanations for why and how organizations come together. Gray and Wood (1991) and Oliver (1990) both identified six concise theoretical perspectives but framed their analyses in large part for organizations operating in the for-profit sector. As such, these studies do not take into consideration the elements that make nonprofit organizations unique and different from their for-profit counterparts—in particular, the mission-driven emphasis of the nonprofit organization. In contrast, Reitan (1998) offered nine distinct theoretical perspectives that assist in understanding strategic alliance formation among nonprofit HSOs. This chapter integrates this literature and offers a new framework of six primary motivating forces that drive the creation and maintenance of strategic alliances among nonprofit HSOs.

Table 2.1
Comparing Nonprofit and For-Profit Theoretical Perspectives of
Interorganizational Relations

For-Profit Theoretical Perspectives (Gray & Wood, 1991)	Nonprofit Theoretical Perspectives
Resource dependence	Resource interdependence
Corporate social performance and institutional economics	Social responsibility
Strategic management and social ecology	Strategic enhancement
Institutional or negotiated order	Environmental validity
Microeconomics	Operational efficiency
Political	Domain influence

Gray and Wood (1991) suggested that the chief motives or rationales for seeking strategic alliances could be understood best in terms of the following six theoretical perspectives: resource dependence, corporate social performance/institutional economics, strategic management/ social ecology, institutional or negotiated order, microeconomics, and political. Reitan (1998) reexamined much of the same organizational theory in relation to human service organizations. This overall framework has been used to analyze merger and consolidation efforts among HSOs and other nonprofit organizations (Yankey et al., 1998). As such, these approaches, once adapted for the special character of nonprofit organizations, provide a useful way of looking at strategic alliance development. Still, for the purposes of this text, it has been important to extend this general framework even further (see Table 2.1).

The following six conceptual themes represent a multifaceted organizing framework involving a range of human service strategic alliances.

Resource Interdependence

The most basic of the six motives for interorganizational activity among HSOs is *resource interdependence.* Its central theme—that partnering offers each member greater access to and opportunity for necessary resources—underpins the other five rationales. Whether any one of the prospective partners needs to depend on the resources of others or all recognize the synergies possible in combining resources, the underlying focus here is on acquiring and/or maintaining resources.

The resources involved are defined broadly and include money, personnel, equipment, expertise, and other things of fundamental value to a particular organization (it is this essential nature of resource interdependence that makes it an underlying current within any of the other theories). Given the competitive nature of resource allocation among HSOs, the acquisition of needed resources can be facilitated by, and often requires, the kind of organizational interreliance that can be achieved through strategic alliances. One frequently noted reason that agencies decide to form an alliance is that they hope to be better able, as a united group, to access funding needed to sustain or expand current services.

The quest for resource interdependence is exemplified in the example of an alliance between a retirement and continuing care facility and a child care agency. The retirement and continuing care facility sought to create an on-site intergenerational child care program that would offer both child care services for staff and an opportunity for residents to work with children for therapeutic and recreational purposes. In the course of investigating funding options, however, the facility identified a significant obstacle. Its executives concluded that it would be too costly for the organization to develop internal expertise in child care, and that funding opportunities were limited without such expertise.

Rather than abandon the goal, the executives decided that a preferable option was to form an alliance with an agency specializing in the provision of child care services. A local agency meeting the facility's criteria was identified. The child care agency was seeking to diversify its funding base, in part, by expanding its range of service delivery options.

The two organizations agreed to jointly coordinate a program that would provide each agency with additional resources to support its own organizational objectives. The initiating organization (the continuing care facility) brought access to a consumer base, space for implementing the program, volunteers to assist the child care providers, and a guaranteed minimum monthly revenue source. The child care agency provided the staff, expertise, accreditation, and educational materials to implement the activities. Despite the substantial resources contributed by each alliance member, full and effective implementation of the program required the interdependence of both participating organizations and their resources.

Social Responsibility

A second easily identifiable rationale for the formation of strategic alliances in the health and human service domains stems from an organization's desire to address a certain community issue or public concern. Organizations motivated by this desire are responding from the perspective of *social responsibility*.

Because the missions of HSOs are generally linked more directly to addressing societal issues than are the missions of their for-profit counterparts, this motivation might seem to be an obvious component of nearly all HSO alliances. However, when the reasons for aligning are thoroughly considered, the desire to address a community issue is often not seen as primary. In the nonprofit sector, social responsibility goes beyond operationalizing the agency's mission. It has to do with the desire to contribute to the resolution of a broad community issue that may not be stated explicitly in the organization's mission. This is one point at which the resource interdependence theme underlying this perspective is evident, as organizations combine their resources to address an issue that none could manage alone as effectively.

Another aspect of the social responsibility framework is the goal of increasing goodwill in the community. In such a case, an organization may establish itself as a member of an alliance to enhance its reputation with its consumers and local residents. By participating in the alliance, the organization can demonstrate to the community that it is concerned about and active in responding to their hopes and expectations for action in a particular area.

For example, in one community, the incidence of adolescent pregnancy was rising to levels that residents considered unacceptable. Several local parent and community groups became vocal about the need for community service providers to do more around pregnancy prevention with local teens. In response, a community-based alliance was formed, beginning with a small, local women's clinic.

The clinic was approached to participate in the alliance by a group of its patients that was concerned about the issue. Looking at the problem from the perspective of social responsibility, the clinic director and staff concluded that they and the agency had valuable resources that would benefit the adolescent pregnancy prevention initiative. The clinic did not specialize in working with adolescents, but it believed the issue was of paramount importance, and it wanted to respond to the expectations of its patients and the broader community for action in this area. Consequently, the clinic joined with 14 other organizations—including local schools, human service providers, government agencies, and businesses—in a collaborative project designed to reduce the incidence of adolescent pregnancy in the community through outreach and education.

Strategic Enhancement

Organizations are motivated by a desire for *strategic enhancement* when they participate in strategic alliances as a means of strengthening their capacity for service delivery, thus gaining market advantage in an increasingly competitive nonprofit environment. Although the concept of competitive advantage may seem counter to the culture of nonprofit organizations, the issues of organizational survival and strengthening strategic position are at the core of this perspective. Of the six models of alliance participation, strategic enhancement is tied most directly to operationalizing the organization's mission.

The assumption behind this perspective is that HSOs exist to address a set of goals directly related to client needs. HSOs may form alliances in order to gain a market edge in meeting those needs. In addition to resource interreliance, they may be seeking to fill a service niche that will permit them to serve more clients or to access additional funding. Or, they may be hoping to increase their opportunities for sustainability and ongoing service provision, thus becoming less dependent on external funding.

Strategic enhancement can include partnership in order to increase the breadth of services that an organization offers. Such service expansion may require the acquisition of additional resources, but when the primary aim of alliance membership is to enhance service delivery or agency survival, the motivation is strategic enhancement.

Consider the example of an alliance between a case management facility and a psychosocial organization largely serving people with severe mental disabilities. Both organizations had excellent community reputations. The psychosocial organization, however, had recently completed a strategic planning process, in the course of which its board of directors concluded that the organization was not prepared to participate effectively in an environment that was increasingly driven by managed care. The organization offered high-quality services that were needed in the community, but it was failing to keep pace with the structural and systems changes necessary to offer these services competitively. A specific area of concern for the organization was that it was not eligible to receive Medicaid reimbursement for services.

The board decided that the best alternative to ensure the survival of its programs was a strategic alliance. It approached the case management facility as a partner because of the facility's strong reputation for being consumer-focused, its access to a wider range of funding sources, and its innovative performance management systems. The alliance successfully created a vehicle through which both organizations were more likely to remain viable in the increasingly competitive service delivery environment. By joining in a strategic alliance of this type, both were able to diversify their funding sources and service delivery options, broaden their client bases, and enhance internal systems.

Operational Efficiency

A fourth organizing framework apparent in the development of HSO partnerships is the perceived need for greater *operational efficiency*. The goal of such an alliance is to improve productivity relative to the available resources in service delivery and/or ongoing operations. Such efforts to increase efficiency can be directed toward reducing duplication of services for a targeted population or any services in a particular program area.

Organizations may seek membership in this type of strategic alliance to enhance the utilization of their resources. This may involve efforts to reduce overhead or service delivery costs. However, although there is a significant focus on resources inherent in this perspective, the fact that the emphasis here is on improving resource usage rather than on gaining access to additional resources makes this rationale consistent with operational efficiency and differentiates it from simply being in the resource interdependence model.

Organizations motivated by operational efficiency also participate in strategic alliances to achieve economies of scale. This is not to imply that bigger always equates with greater efficiency; rather, integrating resources through the combination of programs and/or internal systems such as administration, management information, or evaluation provides more opportunities to create synergistic resource utilization, thus enhancing organizational efficiency.

The co-location of services is one approach that a strategic alliance might consider in response to a desire for operational efficiency. For example, eight HSOs serving a rural farming community formed a partnership to coordinate services for migrant workers. The agencies were all located in the same county, but some were as many as 60 miles from the areas where the workers and their families lived. Staff from each agency made regular trips to the communities to deliver their services to these families. However, these trips did not always coincide with when the families needed the services, and transportation to the agencies' offices was difficult for the families to obtain.

The eight-organization alliance increased the efficiency of service delivery to clients by offering a continuum of services in one conveniently located facility. Clients were then able to obtain child care, education, legal, health care, housing, and counseling services through a single point of access. In addition, the alliance created economies of scale for the member agencies. Instead of having to maintain their own facilities, each of the alliance members now contributed to the cost of maintaining a common facility. They shared equipment and supply costs, as well as several staff members. In this way, they were able to use their limited resources to achieve greater benefits than each could have done individually. One further benefit was that the creation of the single service site streamlined the client referral process and reduced administration and overhead costs for the member agencies.

Environmental Validity

When organizations enter strategic alliances with the overall goal of bolstering their legitimacy with external, institutional stakeholders, they are driven by the need for *environmental validity.* These external, institutional stakeholders, with which HSOs may seek to enhance their credibility, include funders, accrediting bodies, and other organizations operating in their service domain.

Given greater sectorwide competition for resources (monetary and nonmonetary) and the growing need to address a broad range of health and social issues, HSOs must work harder to deliver the quality of service needed to maintain their accountability to multiple stakeholders. Consequently, from the perspective of environmental validity, HSOs are often responding to the expectations of other institutions. Their underlying goal is to maintain or enhance their relationships with these stakeholder organizations in the ongoing pursuit of funding, referrals, or other resources necessary for operationalizing their missions.

Again, there is a relationship between the goal of environmental validity and resource interdependence. When an alliance is formed as a condition of funding or at the recommendation of a potential funder, organizational members are motivated, at least in part, by the desire to maintain a positive reputation with that funder, an action that may help secure future funding or other resources. This focus on legitimacy with the funder is a key distinction between the two motives. In resource interdependence, the sole emphasis is on specific resources.

A second distinguishing feature of environmental validity is that organizations may join alliances from this perspective to strengthen their relationships with specific stakeholder groups or organizations specifically within their service domain. In this case, organizations are striving to exchange information, increase referrals, or enhance organizational visibility with organizations serving similar populations or sharing a common issue focus.

Consider the example of a small HIV/AIDS service agency located on the outskirts of a large, predominantly metropolitan county. It joined a statewide HIV/AIDS awareness alliance in order to enhance its reputation and visibility with external stakeholders. The agency had recently undergone a leadership transition, and its new executive director had been in place only a few months when the agency was informed by a local foundation that one of its grant recipients in the central city was developing an alliance to raise awareness of the need for expanded HIV/AIDS services in the state.

The agency chose to participate in the alliance for several reasons. Certainly, it was interested in engaging in an alliance that focused on public education about HIV/AIDS services. However, the primary motivator for the agency to join the alliance at that time illustrated various aspects of the environmental legitimacy perspective. First, by following up on the information given to the agency by the foundation and demonstrating its willingness to partner with other stakeholders in the HIV/AIDS service arena, the agency was seeking to increase the likelihood of future funding from the foundation. Second, the agency hoped to enhance its own image in the eyes of other larger and more powerful members of the service domain by increasing its visibility and capitalizing on an opportunity to highlight its commitment to addressing shared issues. Finally, with a new executive in the system, the agency was attempting to maintain its established organizational credibility. This effort not only gained the agency greater access to information, but it also served to expedite the new executive's learning curve by stimulating interactions with other, more experienced leaders in the HIV/AIDS service arena.

Domain Influence

One final organizing framework frequently overlooked in attempts to understand the impetus to form or join strategic alliances among HSOs is the framework of *domain influence*. From this perspective, motives of power and control are considered in the broadest sense. More specifically, they center on an agency's desire to increase its organizational strength and/or control in order to safeguard agency interests. In this sense, the agency is seeking to expand its political base. To the extent that power and control are considered resources to an organization, the relationship between the frameworks of domain influence and resource interdependence is clear—organizations can support each other and themselves through an interreliance on individually (and jointly) held areas of domain influence.

In the nonprofit sector, it may be less likely that an organization will openly articulate its desire to increase its power and control than would be the case in the for-profit sector. Moreover, although the terms *power* and *control* sometimes have negative connotations among HSOs, the political motivation for participation in a strategic alliance need not be considered bad. The uniting of member organizations through coadunation—that is, merger or consolidation—is one way to create a single larger and, ideally, stronger and more sustainable organization. Moreover, the desire to exert greater influence in the public policy arena—coupled with the premise that there is power in numbers—is certainly a motive behind the formation of many advocacy coalitions.

An instructive example of the political framework is found in the story of one mid-sized, local behavioral health organization's transformation into a large, regionally based organization through a series of consecutive mergers.

As part of its strategic plan, the board of the behavioral health organization decided that, over the next 5-year period, it needed to more than double its size and range of services. This was not because the organization was responding to a perceived threat to its survival from competitors. Rather, it aimed to become a more powerful organization in the community, and thus have a more feasible chance of effecting systemic change in the way behavioral health services were being delivered in the area. One articulated goal of this growth plan was to strengthen the organization's ability to shape behavioral health policy at the state and national levels. By initiating a series of four consecutive mergers, the organization achieved both its growth objective and a more powerful statewide presence.

ORGANIZING IN NEW DIRECTIONS

To date, comparative research on the motivational underpinnings of alliance formation is still limited. Studies of strategic alliances tend to center more on the general development of specific alliance models rather than the exploration of similarities or differences in the motives, or preconditions, that bring organizations in different types of alliances together. However, one recent national study that examined the strategic alliance experiences of nonprofit organizations included just such an analysis of motivating forces (Yankey, Koney, Bailey, & Wester, 1999).

Overall, the study found that the motivating factors for organizations entering alliances that were characterized by cooperation, coordination, and collaboration were similar; they differed considerably, however, for organizations that chose to coadunate. When organizations coadunate, they create highly formal and interdependent alliances in response to different motivating factors from those of their less formally minded counterparts (Yankey et al., 1999).

Compared to less formal alliances, the more formal and interdependent alliances—that is, coadunating alliances such as mergers and consolidations—tended to be precipitated by factors that were more closely aligned with organizational survival. Regardless of the theoretical perspective under which the alliance was formed, a common theme throughout the experiences of organizations entering into mergers and consolidations was the emphasis on internal, organization-focused goals. Where mergers and consolidations were concerned, the four primary motivating factors describing the organizations' experiences—strategic enhancement, operational efficiency, resource interdependence, and domain influence—were directed at improving opportunities for organizational sustainability in some way. The emphasis on strengthening or improving the operations of the organizations through the coadunation process thus mitigated the possible risks for the organizations in relinquishing their autonomy.

On the other hand, less formal alliances were more often motivated by externally focused or broader environmental factors. The creation of affiliations, associations, and other alliances based on cooperation, coordination, and collaboration were motivated more often by the quest for social responsibility or environmental legitimacy. In contrast to the driving forces behind coadunating alliances, the core issues behind these less formal alliances had more to do with the desire to respond to public needs and expectations. Even when the rationale for such alliances was strategic enhancement, the overriding concern was clearly on enhancing service delivery, not on ensuring organizational survival. Because they were not struggling for organizational survival, these organizations seem to have felt less pressure to enter a partnership that might result in loss of autonomy or identity. Instead, they were able to pursue less restrictive models that would allow them to both accomplish their goals and retain some measure of autonomy and organizational identity.

Chapter 3

DEVELOPING ALLIANCES

Strategic alliances, however fervently or uneasily organizations seek them, do not just happen. Putting one together requires thought and patience. In fact, every alliance has eight different components, each of which requires focused attention. These eight aspects, or building blocks, of an alliance are (a) leadership, (b) membership, (c) environmental linkages, (d) purpose, (e) strategies, (f) tasks, (g) structure, and (h) systems.

This chapter discusses these components and briefly describes the parts they play in a successful partnership. It also demonstrates how these components function in the evolution of an alliance. Every strategic alliance passes through four phases, each of which brings with it its own special challenges and considerations. This chapter provides some questions for alliances to consider as they move through these phases.

THE EIGHT BUILDING BLOCKS OF AN ALLIANCE

There are many ways to think about the multiple pieces that go into making an alliance. For example, Flynn and Harbin (1987) identified five dynamic dimensions that are involved in interagency coordination: climate, resources, policies, people, and process. For Mattessich and Monsey (1992), the crucial elements are the environment, membership, process and structure, communications, purpose, and resources.

This book builds on the work of these and other authors, suggesting a framework for thinking about alliance building. There are three features of this framework that differentiate it from the others:

1. Although strategic alliance research focuses on organizations, the implementation of interorganizational efforts has as much to do with individual relationships. For this reason, it is important to emphasize the human and organizational elements of the process by distinguishing among leadership, membership, and environmental linkages.
2. Resources, policies, and communications are considered along with other necessary systems, such as decision making and evaluation.
3. The strategic alliance process itself is not considered a distinct component. Instead, the way the components are operationalized as a whole in any given alliance determines to what extent that process is unique.

The eight components of strategic alliances are its building blocks. They are the interconnected elements that, taken together, comprise the alliance. However, they do not offer a prescription for how to create a strategic alliance. Instead, they provide the alliance with a set of benchmarks to which it can refer along the way—a comprehensive list of key internal and external factors that can affect the potential success or failure of the alliance.

Leadership and *membership* are two of the first things that should be considered in the formation of a strategic alliance. The leadership of an alliance consists of the individuals and/or organizations that direct and monitor its activities. The remaining participants in the alliance constitute its membership. Alliance members are the organizational and/or individual participants who commit to working with the leaders to accomplish the alliance's goals.

Both components have to be examined on two levels: organizational and individual. In addition, two kinds of leaders affect the development of the alliance: formal (legitimate and stated) and emergent (informal and implied). These multiple levels of leadership and membership are important because each of the leader and member organizations brings a particular culture and set of resources to the alliance that help to define it. In much the same way, the individuals that represent these organizations make the alliance and how it functions unique.

The interaction between leaders and members provides some of the energy that is essential for creating the alliance and sustaining it. The interaction between the alliance and its external stakeholders (members of the community who have a vested interest in the alliance) creates its *environmental linkages*. Environmental linkages infuse the alliance with a second level of energy for accomplishing its purpose.

The organizations and individuals involved in these linkages have an established relationship with the alliance but are not formal members of it. Instead, they provide support for its efforts by, for example, donating meeting space, providing funding, or referring consumers. More broadly, environmental linkages also establish the context for the strategic alliance. They contain much of the history of the community, its needs, and the attempts to meet those needs, and they can often identify which forces in the external environment support or oppose the development of strategic alliances in general or the current alliance in particular.

The *purpose* of the alliance is articulated through its shared values, mission, and goals. The alliance's purpose is whatever it is seeking to achieve through joint activity. *Strategies* are the broad means and methods through which the alliance seeks to facilitate the achievement of the alliance purpose, and *tasks* are the specific activities that collectively enable the alliance to accomplish its purpose and operationalize its strategies.

Structure is the way that the people and tasks are organized within the alliance. Structural characteristics include the assignment of functions and services, where leaders and members are geographically located in relation to each other, committee arrangements, the degree to which decision making is centralized (in one or more committees and/or with one or more organizations or people), and the extent to which policies and procedures are formally defined.

Finally, *systems* are the operating ties that hold the structure together. To have effective decision making, information flow, resource allocation, planning, personnel management, and evaluation, each of these activities must have its own system and specific set of mechanisms defining it. However, they must all work together smoothly for the sake of the whole.

As is suggested by their definitions, the eight alliance components of leadership, membership, linkages, purpose, tasks, strategies, structure, and systems are dynamic and interdependent. Although strength in one component may help compensate for weaknesses in others, it is important to recognize that all alliance components need to function effectively for the alliance to thrive. Leaders and members also need to be aware that a change in any one component affects the others—sometimes obviously, sometimes more subtly. Because the way in which these components are defined operationalizes the alliance process, strengths or weaknesses in any of these components, as well as changes that are made in any of them, affect the evolution of the alliance. Therefore, a successful alliance not only recognizes the interconnection of the components and the process, but also makes time to continually assess how they are working together to make the alliance the best that it can be.

HOW HSO ALLIANCES DEVELOP

The evolution of HSO alliances, as expected, has some things in common with the life cycles of individual organizations and other small groups. So, looking at what is known about their development can help organizations better understand what goes on with these partnerships.

Researchers have identified multiphase life cycle models to track the evolution of single organizations and groups (Adizes, 1979; Hasenfeld & Schmid, 1989; Perlmutter, 1990; Tuckman & Jensen, 1977). Related studies have analyzed developmental issues such as the alignment of leadership and membership needs (Bailey & Grochau, 1993); relationships between environmental and organizational changes (Lawrence & Lorsch, 1969; Tichy, 1987); the roles of structure and planning (Gray & Ariss, 1985; Kanter, Stein, & Jick, 1992; Schein, 1987); and linkages among systems, purpose, and tasks (Beckhard & Harris, 1987).

These studies have provided the basis for looking at the life cycles of strategic alliances in a more systematic way. Some of the researchers who have examined the evolution of interorganizational alliances see them as evolving in three phases, some in as many as five. Gray (1989) and the Synergos Institute (1992) have proposed three-phase models.

In each, the first phase of the alliance's life focuses on defining the focal issue and securing the involvement of its members. In the second phase, the alliance negotiates the parameters of work, including the roles and responsibilities of individual members, and then implements the activities that are necessary to accomplish its goals. In the third, and final, phase, the alliance focuses on evaluating and institutionalizing the alliance effort.

Existing four- and five-phase models of alliance development recognize the same fundamental tasks but include additional critical periods that are characterized by activities such as building trust and strategic planning (Melaville & Blank, 1993); the development of systems and plans (Flynn & Harbin, 1987; Kagan, 1991); or, in some cases, termination (Rosenthal & Mizrahi, 1994).

All of these frameworks, however, have four things in common. First, each framework sees the alliance's evolution as developmental. The phases build on each other. As in human development, the resolution of issues in earlier phases facilitates the successful negotiation of issues in subsequent phases. Yet the process is also iterative. It involves both repetition and occasionally revisiting certain issues. While moving along the path of its evolution, the alliance may need to look backward from time to time to see where it has been or to revisit some issue it thought it had already resolved. It is important to allow for changes from within or outside an alliance that may require the alliance to revisit a previously completed phase.

Second, the fact that an alliance has been together for a long time does not necessarily mean that it will have reached a late phase of development. Although more mature organizations and alliances often have different needs from their newer counterparts, both may face common issues and, correspondingly, find themselves working on the same developmental phase.

Third, each of the phases presented in these frameworks is characterized by certain activities that distinguish it from preceding or subsequent phases. The kinds of activities in which an alliance is engaged provide a good clue to where it is in its development.

Sometimes, an alliance may even appear to be operating in two phases at once. This can occur, for example, when funding mandates necessitate the delivery of services prior to the alliance finalizing its structure and systems, or when an alliance that has been operating for a long time must suddenly address the need for new members. When this happens, it is important to remember that each phase builds on the previous one and that appropriate attention is needed to resolve the alliance issues regardless of whether they are characteristic of a previous phase.

Finally, these frameworks consider both the internal and environmental life of the alliance and raise considerations on both fronts, such as decision-making strategies (internal) and building community support (external), that have implications for the partnership's development.

The alliance development framework presented here consists of phases that originated from research on consortia (Bailey & Koney, 1995a). However, further study suggested that these phases were applicable to the broader continuum of HSO strategic alliances. Building on its predecessors, this framework emphasizes relational aspects, such as trust building among partners, as well as the more practical aspects of assessing the

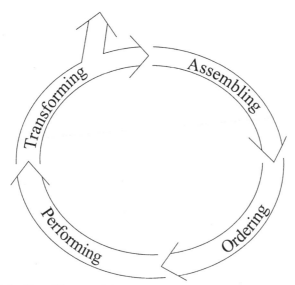

Figure 3.1. Four Phases of Strategic Alliance Development

compatibility of the partners and how successfully the work of the alliance has been systemized.

Under this framework, strategic alliances are seen as going through four developmental phases: (a) *assembling* the member organizations, (b) *ordering* the alliance, (c) *performing* the tasks, and (d) *transforming* the alliance (see Figure 3.1). The critical process and content issues involved in each stage are identified. The framework further suggests areas of transition as the alliance progresses from one phase to the next.

Moving successfully from one phase to the next requires that the alliance leadership focus on both managing the process and critical issues specific to each phase, and negotiating the transition from one phase to the next. Leadership skills and practices that are most effective in facilitating the growth and productivity of the alliance members and the alliance-at-large are highlighted.

However, in general, alliance leaders must pay particular attention to three overriding issues that are part of every phase of the life cycle. These are (a) developing and maintaining trust among members; (b) renewing the commitment of the members to the alliance; and (c) continually monitoring and refining the alliance, its process, and its products.

Assembling: The Art of Getting People Together

The first phase of alliance formation is *assembling*. During this phase, potential partner organizations come together to explore the possibility of an alliance. The first step in the assembling phase generally occurs before organizations actually sit down together. Potential partner organizations, frequently led by the executive director or the board, internally identify themselves as interested in pursuing a possible alliance. At this time, the organization's leaders and its staff should articulate their reasons for seeking to be part of an alliance and the benefits, as they see them, of doing so. They should consider frankly the risks and liabilities in conversations among themselves and with the organization at large.

Part of the task of the organization at this preliminary phase is to identify possible partners and begin exploring with them their interest in forming an alliance. Even if an organization is reacting to the proposal of another organization suggesting that an alliance be considered, it is important that time be spent early on by the individual organizations in thinking through their priorities and goals with regard to participation. Each organization needs to answer at least two key questions in this phase: What do we want to accomplish through participation in the alliance? What are we willing to give up to accomplish this?

Once potential members have come together to discuss the alliance, they engage in conversations ranging from relaxed to intense about what the HSOs have in common and how joint action would benefit each organization and the community. The focus should be on developing trust among partners and beginning to create a set of consciously shared values on which the alliance can be built and sustained.

Although an outside facilitator may be brought in to lead this discussion, the organization (or individual) who initiates an alliance conversation is typically identified at this time as the leader, or the convener. Over time, other individual members or organizations may emerge as the formal leaders of the new partnership, but the initial alliance leader is the one that orchestrates the assembling process.

As leaders emerge, the alliance will need to be reassured of their abilities to maintain equal loyalties to their own organizations and to the partnership. This is critical to the process of continuing to build trust within the alliance. As the alliance members expose their own vulnerabilities, the leader must reassure them that he or she can remain objective and continue to pursue the goals of the prospective alliance over those of the indi-

---

Questions to Be Asked in the Assembling Phase

- What is the overall purpose of the alliance?
- Which organization(s) will serve as the leader(s)? Who will represent the leader(s)?
- Which organizations might share an interest in or be able to bring resources to accomplish the purpose?
- How will potential members be approached about involvement?
- What initial level of representation will be requested from prospective members (e.g., executive, clinical staff, etc.)?
- What expectations do members have of each other? Organizationally? Individually?
- What resources might the alliance need to accomplish its purpose?
- What resources can each member bring to the alliance?
- What does each member expect from the alliance? What are the benefits of participation?
- What other information do members want or need to know about each other or the alliance before they will commit to participation?
- What are the costs of participation? What is each member willing to give up to achieve the alliance's purpose?
- Which possible alliance structures would fit best with the purpose, leadership, and membership characteristics of the alliance?
- How will organizational representatives keep their home organizations informed as to the process of the alliance?
- Does the membership represent the diversity of the issue and/or community on which the alliance is focused?

---

vidual member organizations. The leader can do this by creating a shared vision among the members and by attending promptly to the alliance's needs.

It does not matter whether the leadership is composed of one or more organizations or individuals, or whether the leadership style being used is participatory or authoritative—what matters is that here, effective leadership must be inspirational. It must also be practical in that it is always paying attention to the developmental phases of the alliance and the critical issues that arise in each.

Similarly, the membership of the alliance may be composed of individuals and/or organizations. Members may come to an alliance representing a variety of constituencies (e.g., an agency or business, or the members of another strategic alliance). In addition, all members, whether individuals or organizations, will bring different resources and perspectives. This diversity brings strength to an alliance, but it also poses challenges for an alliance, its leader(s), and its members.

Rosenthal and Mizrahi (1994) identified the challenge of "autonomy versus accountability" (p. 119) as a source of dynamic tension among the members of an alliance and an important issue for the alliance as a whole to address. Individual members must have appropriate organizational authority to make decisions within the alliance without having to constantly consult with their organization to resolve all issues. This is not solely to be more efficient and expedite the process. Empowered members are usually better informed about their organizations and thus are better at representing them in the alliance. This does not mean that executive directors or board members must represent organizations in all alliances. Rather, it implies that the organization needs to consider the fit between the organizational representatives to an alliance and the tasks of the alliance. When an organizational representative does not have decision-making authority on behalf of the organization, systems need to be put in place to ensure that both the individual and the alliance are supported.

For some individual members, other issues may arise. Individual alliance members often find it harder than they thought it would be to move from the level of self- and organizational interest to the alliance's best interest. It is often difficult to bring the same enthusiasm and commitment to a new set of priorities that is not necessarily one's own. However, this issue of "mixed loyalties" (Rosenthal & Mizrahi, 1994, p. 119) must be addressed for the alliance to be a success.

In addition, the power ascribed to an individual as a member of an alliance may be equated initially to the credentials or resources of the organization that he or she represents. The converse also may occur. Certain individual members may be trusted more by or be more visible in the community, and thus be seen as more powerful in the alliance. These and other membership differences, such as differences in commitment and contribution levels, characterize the potential challenge of "unity and diversity" (Rosenthal & Mizrahi, 1994, p. 121) and must be acknowledged by the leader and addressed by the alliance as a whole throughout its development.

Although some of these issues may emerge as time goes by, it is best to try to identify these potentially problematic issues at the point of assembling. However, notwithstanding their organizational linkages, it is important to remember that the members of the alliance have been brought together by common issues. It is these shared concerns that form the basis for this framework and will help the members of the alliance negotiate their differences.

The convening leader must take the responsibility of helping potential partners articulate the overall purpose of the alliance and begin to identify the resources necessary to fulfill this purpose. Leaders and members should explore together the possible roles and responsibilities of the individual member organizations, as well as conflicting loyalties that could arise between them and this new union. The leader must try to remain neutral when the group is wrestling with a decision, not allowing her or his organization's needs to be given precedence over the needs of the other members of the alliance.

Sometimes, the leader takes the primary role in identifying the issues that the alliance will address. Such a leader may even be self-appointed. On other occasions, an externally imposed mandate (e.g., a directive from a funder) determines the alliance focus and/or who will hold the leadership position. In still other instances, the leader is selected from among the potential alliance members or the community by those who are concerned about the issues. As a result, the legitimacy of the alliance leader is usually assumed.

Two types of leadership power often characterize alliance leaders. Those who are considered by the members to have special knowledge that qualifies them for leadership are said to possess the power of the expert. Leaders possessing referent power are those with whom members identify for any of a variety of reasons (French & Raven, 1959). However, these initial assumptions must (and will) be tested often over time.

All of the partners must articulate clearly their expectations of the alliance as an important part of the trust-building process. Similarly, any anticipated linkages between the alliance and the members, or between the members and their parent organizations or constituencies, need to be spelled out clearly at this stage. Failure to create a mutual agreement with regard to who is going to be responsible for what and who will be reporting to whom can result in role ambiguity among members, which, in turn, may lead to actions motivated by self-interest rather than the best interests of the alliance. In many ways, this fundamental set of understandings establishes the core energy of an alliance, and it requires constant vigilance because it may be counter to the nature of organizations to share their ideas, goals, and strategies in a competitive market.

As the alliance transitions from the assembling phase to the ordering phase of development, issues requiring special attention will emerge. These transition themes can be identified from the dialogue among members and leaders as they attempt to specify the alliance's tasks and the costs and benefits of membership. The leader of the process must note the areas of perceived agreement and disagreement among the stakeholders and anticipate how these will affect alliance decision making. He or she must be sensitive to the needs and vulnerabilities of each member and facilitate conversations about the possible long-term impacts of the alliance's activities.

Taking Time to Make Sure It Is All Legal

It is during this transition from assembling to ordering that the leaders of the budding alliance and the leaders of the individual organizations—still trying to decide whether and how to come together—must take stock of the legal environment within which they operate. The framework of laws that prescribes the structure and governs the operation of nonprofit, tax-exempt organizations may suggest outlines for, or impose constraints upon, how the alliance should be constructed and how it should undertake to carry out its mission.

These issues are weightier where more formal alliances are being contemplated, but it is safe to say that legal advice from someone with expertise in state nonprofit corporation law and federal tax exemption law is an essential ingredient from this point forward. Even at the less formal end of the alliance spectrum, the prospect of an alliance may raise legal issues that, if not carefully attended to in the planning stages, have the potential to become legal problems later. For example, in one of the cases described in this book, the alliance had to modify its advocacy focus to comply with the requirements of grant funding it received.

In addition, laws and regulations that pertain to specific areas of operation have been changing over the past several years and may have an increasing role in determining how alliances should be structured and operated. Such laws and regulations need to be investigated prior to formalizing the alliance systems and structure. Examples include low-income housing laws related to a neighborhood redevelopment organization or alliance; Medicare regulations and federal and state hospital, nursing home, or home health services regulations for a health care organization or alliance; and federal, state, and local funding and licensing laws and regulations, where a child day care organization or alliance is being contemplated.

The legal dimensions of structure and operation must be considered at two levels: (a) the individual organization contemplating participation in the alliance, and (b) the alliance itself. The leaders of the individual organization must assess whether the proposed alliance participation is consistent with the legal constraints under which the organization currently operates. If not, the organization may need to seek to rearrange those constraints that are within its power to alter, reconceive the structure and operation of the proposed alliance or the nature of the organization's participation to bring them into line with the organization's legal constraints, or abandon the idea of participating in the alliance. At the alliance level, an appropriate legal form must be chosen, and organizational documents, such as articles of incorporation, bylaws, and application for federal tax exemption, if appropriate, must be generated. Although these are actually activities associated with the ordering phase of development, ideally, the alliance will have established a relatively clear understanding of these legal ramifications before moving fully into this phase.

The organization contemplating participation in an alliance must consider whether its proposed involvement is compatible with its purpose, as spelled out in its articles of incorporation; its bylaws; and any documents, if such exist, that establish a relationship with a parent organization. These sources of the organization's own internal rules will also prescribe the process for making and implementing the decision of whether to enter the alliance, as well as identify who may make the decision for the organization. In some organizations, this will be the board; in others, the decision may have to be approved by the executive director, the staff, or a parent organization.

Under the principles of state charitable trust law, an organization's assets may be bound by explicit or implicit restrictions that prevent their shift to new uses in connection with, for example, an alliance's pursuits. If the contemplated alliance calls for redirection of organizational assets, it may be necessary to consult with the state's attorney general, or even to seek court approval of the shift.

Several areas of federal tax exemption law may need to be considered. First among these is whether the contemplated participation in the alliance is consistent with the organization's tax-exempt status. If participation in the alliance takes the organization into new charitable territory, the change must be reported on the organization's annual information return to the Internal Revenue Service (IRS). If the alliance will be engaging in activity that might be considered "commercial" in the eyes of the IRS, the organization must consider whether the activity will be attributed to the participants and, if so, whether it might threaten the organization's qualification for tax exemption.

Participation in joint venture arrangements raises particularly complex tax exemption issues; choices made about the legal structure of the joint venture can mean the difference between continued qualification for exemption and loss of tax-exempt status. If the alliance's activities are expected to generate revenue for its participating organizations, it is necessary to consider whether the revenues will be taxable as unrelated business income and whether impact of the income on the organization's mix of revenues will affect its status as a public charity as opposed to a private foundation.

If the alliance is expected to engage in advocacy work, the organization must consider whether lobbying efforts or political intervention by representatives of the alliance may be attributed to the individual member organizations, thus jeopardizing their individual organizations' tax-exempt status. Conversely, participation in the alliance, if structured correctly, may expand an organization's opportunities to influence policy.

Not all of these considerations are relevant to every planned alliance. Some alliances require no more than a scan of the legal context to determine that none of these issues is germane. But even if some or all of the issues described here loom as potential problems, they need not become barriers to proceeding. Identifying which, if any, are relevant to the actual circumstances at hand and attending to them prospectively is simply a necessary part of this early stage of development.

In fact, careful consideration of the legal aspects of participation in the alliance is just one dimension of the fiduciary obligation of the organization's leaders. In governing a nonprofit corporation, its board of directors or officers are bound by a duty of loyalty and a duty of care. They must act in good faith, in the best interest of the organization, and with informed judgment. Duty of loyalty demands that an organization's leaders do not subordinate the organization's interests to their own or to those of other participants or the alliance itself; if the alliance structure contemplates overlapping boards, consideration must be given to whether the overlap may create untenable conflicts of interest. Duty of care demands that the organization's decision makers diligently seek out and carefully consider sufficient information upon which to base a good-faith judgment about whether to participate in the alliance. The nature and extent of information that is considered sufficient will necessarily vary, depending on the nature and circumstances of the contemplated alliance.

Really Getting to Know Your Partner:
A Few Words About Due Diligence

Due diligence, a concept that originated in the for-profit sector, involves "the systematic investigation of an organization's operations" (McLaughlin, 1998, p. 174), and it is also central to the transition from assembling to ordering, especially where more formal alliances, such as mergers and consolidations, are being contemplated. Yet a form of due diligence should be a part of the evolutionary process regardless of the alliance's formality. The due diligence process focuses predominantly on assessing a potential partner's legal and financial status in order to determine potential liabilities that may be brought into the alliance, but the process also compares organizations to ascertain where efficiencies can be achieved, and, where nonprofit organizations are involved, it should include the identification of divergences in values among the members.

Due diligence is particularly important in mergers and consolidations, because once the coadunation process is complete, the assets and liabilities of the member organizations are combined. Consequently, nonprofit organizations frequently rely on external legal and/or financial counsel to complete this process. The essence of due diligence, however, is to learn as much about one's potential partners as possible before fully engaging in an alliance with them. This principle applies in the formation of any alliance, but in less formal alliances, the process is less often officially prescribed. This is because, in cooperation, coordination, and, to a large extent, collaboration, members retain most of their organizational autonomy, and liabilities are not intertwined.

Nevertheless, assessing the compatibility of potential partners as thoroughly as possible is a fundamental element of the trust-building process. The more partners know about each other, the less likely it is that organizational surprises will cause serious conflict among members and threaten the survival of the alliance in the future. Ideally, with all of this work completed, the alliance is ready to move to the second developmental phase.

Ordering: Do All of the Pieces Work Together?

In the *ordering* phase, operational issues involving the differentiation and integration of systems, strategies, and structure emerge. It is now the responsibility of the leader to ensure that these organizational components are sufficiently understood so that their parts are recognized as clearly delineated but also interconnected. The leader must now also aid members in establishing norms for conflict management and creating mechanisms for determining the new rules and regulations as they relate to the tasks necessary to achieve the alliance's purpose. Systems that provide for the distribution of resources garnered by the alliance, the flow of information, and task evaluation must be discussed and decided on at this time.

During the ordering phase, discussions can be intense, alternating from the politely formal to the suddenly explosive when the partners are brought face-to-face with the new reality. The ordering phase is also a time when organizations spend a considerable amount of time writing things down to document issues of importance to them and how the alliance will operate. This level and type of emotionality, coupled with a clearer sense of the costs of the new alliance, may lead some of the original members to leave.

Although alliances can break down at any point in the life cycle, many end at this time. A common reason for this is that organizations are not able to develop enough trust among themselves to tackle the difficult issues. Protecting organizational turf often takes precedence over determining what is best for the alliance and all of its stakeholders. If alliance members are able to negotiate these issues and the development process continues, membership issues may again become important as this turnover occurs and dialogues with new organizations begin taking place to ensure that the alliance sustains itself and expands its base of resources.

Another important consideration in ordering the alliance is creating an appropriate structure. The alliance must work to establish normative procedures and design systems for operationalizing its purpose and strategies. At this point, conversations about the alliance move from the conceptual to the practical. As the actual implementation of activity becomes a reality, unexpected challenges are often presented by an ever-present fact: the idiosyncrasies of human nature. The alliance and its

Questions to Be Asked in the Ordering Phase

- How will the alliance and its members achieve their purpose? What strategies will they implement? What tasks will they undertake?
- What additional resources will the alliance need?
- What resources will each member commit to contributing to the alliance?
- How will the alliance secure other resources?
- How will the alliance's total resources be used? Will they be divided among the member organizations? If so, how?
- What is the most appropriate structural model for the alliance?
- What activities are required by law to structure the alliance?
- What policies are needed to document alliance systems?
- What agreements are necessary to document members' roles and responsibilities?
- Will the alliance obtain legal counsel on its contracts, issues, and recommendations? If so, how?
- Who will be the alliance's leader(s)? Will leadership be shared? Will it rotate?
- How will the alliance be governed?
- How will planning and administration of the alliance be coordinated?
- How will alliance decisions be made? How will the alliance manage consensus and conflict?
- What committees will be needed to support decision making and oversee or implement alliance strategies?
- Do organizational representatives have sufficient autonomy to make decisions on behalf of their organizations?
- Do certain decisions need to be reviewed at other levels of the member organizations before the alliance acts on them? How will this process be handled?
- Do representatives from other levels of the member organizations need to be involved in the alliance? If so, how?

(continued)

Questions to Be Asked in the Ordering Phase (Continued)

- What information will be disseminated to alliance members? To alliance stakeholders? How will it be disseminated?
- What staff are needed to carry out the alliance's strategies and tasks? Will staff time be contributed by the members? Will staff be hired or paid for by the alliance?
- How will staff be supervised? By the alliance leader? Specific members? Others?
- How will the alliance evaluate its process? What are the desired outcomes? How will issues be identified and continuous improvement be facilitated? How will interim successes be celebrated?
- Are new members needed? How will new members be recruited and oriented?
- How will the voices of consumers and other stakeholders be included in the alliance?
- What community linkages does the alliance need to accomplish its purpose?
- What other information do members want or need to continue their work?

members must remain flexible so that they can identify and manage these challenges effectively, while at the same time accomplishing the primary developmental tasks of this phase.

During the ordering phase, the alliance must begin to reconcile desires for control with the need to include others. Most of the norms to be established focus on either decision making or managing consensus and conflict. It is at this point that the question of the legal structure of the alliance must be resolved. If the alliance being formed requires modifications to the member organizations' legal or tax-exempt status, the necessary steps need to be undertaken to begin this process.

As the alliance begins to move from ordering to performing, the transition themes now focus on protecting the resources of the alliance and its activities from external interference. Concurrently, the leader must concentrate on strengthening (or rediscovering) the alliance's internal vitality, creative energy, and sense of purpose, which may have been dampened by the establishment of formal policies and procedures. The leader must help the members avoid "group think" (Janis, 1972, p. 9)—that is, the trap of agreeing with one another just to maintain harmony—by helping the group explore alternatives and challenging the members to avoid reaching closure on an issue prematurely. Such discussions allow the alliance to perform the tasks that are necessary to accomplish the goals while maintaining each organization's individual mission.

Performing: The Move From Strategy to Action

As the alliance moves into the *performing* phase, it must now turn its attention outward. But for it to be able to do so, the alliance leaders and members must understand clearly the costs and benefits of membership, their new roles, and how they fit into the larger context. They must also have agreed to place a higher value on the good of the alliance than solely on the benefits to their own constituencies. The majority of a leader's efforts in this phase are directed toward assisting the members in operationalizing the various systems that have been established to accomplish the alliance's goals. These actions are critical to executing the specific tasks of the alliance.

In this phase, energy is expended on performance and activity rather than on planning. With the work of the alliance now in progress, communication among the total membership is often considered less important, with organizations coming together to exchange information only as necessary. However, it is vital that the leader strive to keep all systems moving and all parties informed so that organizational subgroups do not emerge and members do not feel excluded.

With the alliance actively performing its tasks, fewer official meetings of all of the members will probably be held. Communications among partners tend to be written now, with the leader monitoring the effectiveness of systems, strategies, and structure that were defined earlier. Periodic check-ins to make sure everyone is aware of what is happening throughout the alliance and to address issues as they arise are helpful here. Opportunities for members to acknowledge progress and setbacks must be made, and this information can be used to enhance relationships

---

Questions to Be Asked in the Performing Phase

- How are tasks divided among members? Among staff? Are changes needed?

- Is the leadership supporting the alliance's work? Are changes needed?

- Does the membership continue to be representative of the issue or community on which the alliance is focused? Are changes needed?

- How are members benefiting from participation? What are the costs? Does the benefit-cost ratio support continued member involvement? Are changes needed?

- Is the structure supporting the alliance's work? Are changes needed?

- Are the various systems (decision making, information dissemination, resource development and allocation, etc.) supporting the alliance's work? Are changes needed?

- Are strategies and tasks supporting the accomplishment of the alliance's purpose? Are changes needed?

- With which organizations can the alliance link to strengthen its work?

- What additional resources are needed to implement the alliance's work?

- What interim successes has the alliance achieved?

---

with others (individuals and organizations) outside of the alliance so that they will be willing to support its work.

The legal dimensions of the alliance also must receive ongoing attention, and individual participant organizations must continue to monitor and respond to the impact that alliance activities may have on their own legal situation. For example, revenue-generating activities of the alliance, if such exist, may or may not result in unrelated business taxable income for alliance participants, and alliance lobbying efforts may or may not be attributable to individual member organizations. Focused attention to these aspects of the alliance are essential to prevent surprises that can threaten the viability of the alliance or its member organizations.

The themes that help to transition an alliance from the performing phase to the transforming phase are those that focus on the effectiveness of the alliance's efforts. They lead to an examination of what could be done differently in the future, or the next time. Additional community concerns also are identified at this time.

Transforming: The Alliance Rethinks Itself[1]

At some point in the life of an alliance, the members must formally reassess their commitment to the alliance and determine if and how the alliance will proceed. This *transforming* phase is generally precipitated by a specific event or guideline, such as the accomplishment of the alliance's initial goal or the end of the initial term set for the alliance's work. The transforming phase offers three possibilities for the future of the alliance: (a) The alliance can formally end, (b) the alliance can continue unchanged, or (c) the alliance can change any or all of its components.

A common reason for the alliance to enter the transforming phase is the achievement of its initial goals. In such a case, the alliance may choose to disband, or it may choose to continue its work toward new goals. When the alliance achieves its initially agreed-upon purpose, the leaders and members must choose among the three possible alternatives: ending, continuing unchanged, or reforming and continuing. If the choice is made, for whatever reason, to continue the alliance, the leaders and members will have to cycle back, if only briefly, through the assembling and ordering phases of development.

In this process, they need to revisit the salient issues of each phase. Individual member organizations will need to assess whether the alliance's purpose and activities are still consistent with their own goals, resources, and legal constraints. More formal alliance structures may require legal restructuring at this point.

Regardless of why the alliance has reached the transforming phase, this phase is characterized by change and reflection. The time has come to evaluate the outcomes of the alliance's formation. As will be discussed in Chapter 11, the alliance yields the greatest impact from evaluation if it was clearly defined in the ordering phase and used to provide continuous assessment of the alliance's process and content throughout all phases of development. Now, in the transforming phase, stakeholders informally and formally use the evaluation system established earlier to officially review the effectiveness of the alliance as it moves through transformation. The data collected in this final evaluation are used to inform decisions on how to proceed.

Questions to Be Asked in the Transforming Phase

- Why is the alliance facing a transforming decision now? Has it achieved its purpose?
- Have stakeholders been involved in and informed about the decision to transform the alliance?
- Do members believe that an alliance effort needs to continue?
- If the alliance will continue, how can it best revisit questions and issues raised in the assembling, ordering, and performing phases?
- Will the alliance continue under the same structure, or is a new model more appropriate?
- Will contracts or bylaws require amendment?
- If the alliance will not continue, how can it celebrate successes and the members' contributions? How can it document lessons learned?

Analysis of the successes and challenges of the alliance, however, is only one aspect of the final evaluation process. Even if the alliance did not reach its target goal, the leaders and members must examine the alliance's accomplishments and recognize both their roles in these achievements. Such an assessment must be done publicly and privately and should recognize individual and collective successes.

If the alliance is ending, a temptation once the decision has been made may be to simply stop meeting. Similarly, if the alliance is proceeding unchanged, members may not see the need to reassess the critical issues of the assembling and ordering phases. The primary role of the leadership, however, is to understand the appropriate direction that the alliance must now take and facilitate its transformation, working toward balancing both the current and future needs of the alliance, its members, and its stakeholders.

NOTE

1. In our earlier work, the fourth phase of alliance development was identified as the ending phase. However, working with that language revealed that it obscured the fact that concluding and disbanding an alliance is only *one* of the options available to the alliance in this fourth phase.

Part II

COOPERATION

Mutual Support Without Loss of Autonomy

When organizations begin to think about participating in strategic alliances, they have many structural and process options from which to choose. These alternatives range from loosely connected alliances to those that are very formal and integrated. Each alliance type has its function, and sometimes, there is no need to enter into a complex relationship. Sometimes, organizations merely want to exchange information about a particular issue or client(s). They may simply want to support or endorse one another's efforts or share certain resources, such as mailing lists or special expertise. Perhaps they want to co-sponsor a workshop or other event. These organizations may have no interest in affecting one another's way of operating or providing services, and they may not be willing to sacrifice any of their autonomy to work together.

In such cases, organizations would likely choose to *cooperate* with each other in an alliance such as an affiliation. When organizations cooperate, they remain independent but contribute information and other resources (usually non-monetary) to support each other's activities. Cooperation is the least structured of the four strategic alliance processes and is characterized by low levels of organizational integration and formalization (see Figure P2.1). Because only verbal or informal agreements are normally involved, the creation of a cooperative alliance is not likely to raise legal issues for participants beyond those involved in any new undertaking.

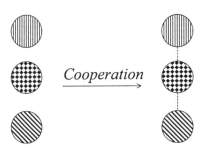

Figure P2.1. Cooperation

The central focus of a cooperative alliance is the recognition of similarities *and* differences among the members of the alliance. A cooperative alliance such as an affiliation can give individual organizational members the opportunity to assess the effectiveness of their operational style or practices in relation to other members' and to learn from them. Organizational self-interest is primary in the decision to participate in a cooperative alliance, and the overriding organizational value is *self-interest in relation to others' interests.*

The focus of activity is in the individual organizations, with each organization using the combined resources of the alliance to implement its own tasks or activities. Minimal consideration is given to how these resources can be used to achieve broader goals beyond information sharing and organizational endorsement.

Decision making in a cooperative alliance is decentralized. In other words, the member organizations retain independent decision-making authority, and decisions made in the context of the alliance generally do not affect the structure or operations of the member organizations, thus limiting the organizational interdependence and the more substantial risks, or costs, associated with more highly integrated alliances. Moreover, members do not lose much, if any, autonomy by participating because the overarching function of the alliance is mutual support. If joint administration of significant funds is going to be involved, the organizations should be contemplating a more highly structured alliance process in which the systems for doing so are defined more formally.

Sometimes, the purpose of the cooperative alliance is to explore the possibility of a more formal alliance. In this case, the outcome of the cooperation will be the decision as to whether to proceed. Thus, no structural or operational changes are needed until the new alliance begins.

When organizations cooperate, the administrative leadership of the alliance is informal, and usually, there is no official governing body. One of the cooperating organizations may be assigned the responsibility of regularly disseminating information or coordinating meetings and activities, or the responsibility for these tasks may rotate among the members. Naturally, the organization that has the more direct access to information or to other resources targeted by the alliance will have a certain measure of power. But issues of power are minimized in cooperative alliances because there is limited risk associated with participation.

The size of a cooperative alliance varies with its specific tasks. If its goal is simply information sharing, it may be quite large; if its purpose is co-sponsoring a workshop, there may be only a few members.

Just as the leadership of the individual members' organizations continues to operate independently, staffing also tends to be uncoordinated. Such staff time as is necessary to accomplish certain tasks is contributed voluntarily by the member organizations, and tasks are divided based on the informal agreements of members. Interorganizational exchanges occur at staff, administrative, or governance levels depending on the task or tasks that the alliance seeks to implement. Few environmental linkages are usually required, because the function of such an alliance is generally not complex enough to require much external support.

Strategies and tasks are directed largely at data gathering and communication. Contact among cooperating organizations takes place as needed to share information. It may range from infrequent to sporadic, depending on the nature of the alliance. Similarly, the duration of a cooperative alliance may be either long-term or quite brief, depending on its purpose.

Chapter 4

AFFILIATIONS

At one end of the continuum of strategic alliances is the *affiliation,* a loosely connected system of two or more organizations with a similar interest or interests. According to one definition, classification of an alliance as an affiliation "requires little more than meetings and good faith" (McLaughlin, 1998, p. 56). However, the core concept of an affiliation is one of mutual support.

Member organizations in an affiliation continue to operate independently while supporting one another through the exchange of information; endorsements; and other, largely nonmonetary resources. This cooperative arrangement provides members with the greatest amount of flexibility in their activities and creates an internal synergy as member organizations disseminate ideas and information.

The term *network* is sometimes used to describe such an alliance (Rosenthal & Mizrahi, 1994; Winer & Ray, 1994). However, in the current environment, this leads to some confusion because network is now used widely in the health care and child welfare arenas to mean something very different. As will be discussed in Chapter 8, the formation of managed care networks necessitated a change in terminology to differentiate less formal networks from more formal ones. As a result, this book describes the least formal of the alliance models as affiliations and reserves the use of the term network to specify a more highly structured interorganizational relationship.

The relationship among organizations in an affiliation is typically nonbinding. Member interactions can range from the formal to the informal depending on the focus of the alliance, but affiliated organizations generally are not obligated by contracts or written commitments to adhere to the alliance's recommendations and decisions. Examples of affiliations include referral networks and event co-sponsorships. The affiliation of Mobile Meals of Toledo (Ohio), Inc. with a community-based nursing association in the Toledo area provides one illustration of how an affiliation might be operationalized.

Mobile Meals of Toledo has two main service programs. Meals on Wheels delivers prepared meals to housebound individuals and families. Mobile Market, a large mobile grocery store, makes weekly visits to housing facilities for seniors, people with disabilities, and low-income residents so that they can do their own shopping without traveling to the grocery store.

In the early 1990s, Mobile Meals of Toledo began to realize that many of its Mobile Market consumers were not consistently taking advantage of available local health care programs. Consistent with its mission, Mobile Meals began investigating ways to help its consumers access these needed services. One of the Mobile Meals of Toledo's board members suggested that the agency contact an area nursing organization that provided flu shots in the community to see if there was a way the organizations might work together. After approximately one year of planning, the two organizations began an affiliation through which nurses delivered flu shots to Mobile Meals of Toledo's consumers in conjunction with the Mobile Market shopping experience.

The affiliation is loosely constructed and operates without a formal structure. It relies primarily on a verbal agreement between the two organizations' executives to cooperate in providing the flu shots each year. The two executives meet each spring to plan the process. They share information by phone and fax throughout the summer, and the shots are delivered to Mobile Market consumers in the fall. Mobile Meals retains all the communication with the consumers and host sites, and its affiliation partner delivers the flu shots and administers the Medicare reimbursement process.

Although affiliations like this one may be focused on a particular task, they may also be a precursor to a more formal alliance. Members in an affiliation have the opportunity to get to know each other better before formalizing their commitments to each other. They can also build trust in a relationship that requires a minimal degree of risk before they agree to put forward additional resources and give up greater autonomy. The Shared Wellness Project exemplifies such an affiliation.

CASE STUDY: **Shared Wellness Project, an Affiliation**
REPORTER: **Ann Arbor YMCA**

—OVERVIEW

The Shared Wellness Project is a public-private affiliation of the Ann Arbor (Michigan) YMCA, an area hospital, and a local community college. The affiliation is in its second iteration. It began as a cooperative effort to study the possibility of the three organizations jointly creating and providing comprehensive wellness and fitness programs in a central facility. After the affiliation accomplished this goal and entered the transforming phase of development, its members elected to continue the affiliation with a new, albeit related, purpose. Once the members decided to proceed, the alliance evolved into an affiliation focused on completing a feasibility study for a wellness facility and developing a plan to jointly provide recreational, educational, and rehabilitation programs to benefit its members' employees and consumers as well as other county residents.

—PRECONDITIONS

The Shared Wellness Project began when the Ann Arbor YMCA, the hospital, and the college acknowledged the similarity in their goals related to enhancing community health and wellness services and the inherent difficulty each would have in fully achieving its goal on its own. The three member organizations had individually identified goals aimed at increasing their respective health and wellness services and recognized the need for new or enhanced facilities in which to offer them.

Impetus for the alliance came from the organizations' trustees. The three organizations shared several trustees and six policy volunteers, who served as members of development committees and other decision-making groups. The volunteers were aware of the organizations' compatible goals and knew what obstacles each faced in trying to accomplish these goals.

Prior to the formation of the alliance, the Ann Arbor YMCA did not hold a strong position in the community. For several years, the YMCA had administrative and financial difficulties that had weakened its community image. In addition, although the organization provided a range of fitness and recreational programs in central Ann Arbor, this narrow geographic focus limited its consumer base. When the YMCA hired a new executive director in the mid-1990s, the organization was ready to begin forming strategic alliances. New to the community and the YMCA, the executive director was concerned about the organization's survival and sought ways to broaden its delivery of health and recreation services beyond central Ann Arbor to increase the organization's visibility and viability. Developing alliances with other organizations presented a way to accomplish this.

At the same time, the hospital's leaders wanted to improve the cost-effectiveness of their rehabilitation services. They were also interested in expanding their business to include wellness programs and in finding a way to increase the number of people served by their health education efforts. Similarly, the college wanted to enhance its curriculum by providing physical education instruction and sought to give students greater access to recreational and fitness programs outside the curriculum. In addition, the college recognized the need to champion wellness initiatives for its faculty and staff. One challenge that the college faced in accomplishing its goals was securing a facility in which to offer these programs.

The trustees and policy volunteers who worked with the three organizations were able to see the potential for the development of an alliance. The volunteers shared this information with the chief administrators of the three organizations and recommended that they meet to discuss the similarity of their interests. The full boards of the organizations were not involved in this decision, but they were aware that a process was beginning.

—PROCESS #1

In late 1995, the presidents of the college and the hospital met with the YMCA's executive director to explore the compatibility of their goals around enhancing health and wellness. They also discussed the idea of establishing a jointly held facility in which to deliver these services. The organizations concurred that sharing in the development of one facility would enhance their programs, and collective implementation would produce benefits beyond what each could achieve individually. Each of the executives endorsed the idea of pursuing the alliance, which later was named the Shared Wellness Project. By February 1996, the members had formed an affiliation and begun to explore the project in more depth.

The organizational members were the three initiating organizations: Ann Arbor YMCA, the hospital, and the college. The three organizations brought their own expertise related to health and wellness to the alliance. The college is a large, public institution with more than 1,000 employees, and the hospital is a large, private institution that is part of a larger hospital system and employs nearly 5,000 people. The hospital and college had worked together in the past, in part because of their geographic proximity. They were located on adjacent properties, and with the potential for locating the wellness facility on their land, the two organizations offered more than financial and informational resources to the alliance. In contrast, the Ann Arbor YMCA is a small, community-based organization with a small staff. However, the YMCA and its national association have strong reputations for providing a wide range of community-based fitness and recreational programs as well as a demonstrated history of developing and operating facilities in which such programs are offered.

The purpose of the initial affiliation was to explore the idea of a more structured alliance focusing on the joint promotion of health and wellness. The primary strategy was to conduct a needs assessment on the possibility of creating a new facility in which to locate these activities. The leaders created two committees to structure the affiliation and accomplish this goal. These committees were the policy committee and the exploratory committee.

The executives of the three member organizations comprised the policy committee. The committee met quarterly to discuss issues related to project oversight and coordination. The three executives shared leadership of the affiliation through this committee. The hospital president chaired the meetings, although each organizational executive had an equal vote. The leadership style was participatory and responsive to the needs and concerns of its organizational members. Less formally, the leadership of the alliance shifted from one organization to another depending on the importance of the issue to each member. There were no formal contracts or agreements committing the organizations to work together. Consistent with the nature of an affiliation, informal agreements among the executives governed the participation of member organizations in the alliance.

Members of the exploratory committee were the executive director and a board member of the YMCA, two administrative representatives from the college, and three administrative representatives from the hospital. The executive director of the YMCA chaired this committee, which met monthly and carried out the majority of the affiliation's tasks.

Using a work outline prepared by the policy committee to frame its activities, the exploratory committee divided the necessary tasks among its members, with the YMCA taking the lead on many of the activities. The committee met for 9 months to accomplish its specified tasks.

—OUTCOMES #1

The exploratory committee documented the alliance's purpose through the development of a vision statement. It completed a preliminary needs assessment, investigating community demographics and existing programs offering related services in the target community. The committee explored similar health and wellness partnerships nationally, looking specifically at those in which a YMCA aligned with a hospital or college, and drafted a concept summary for the development of a shared wellness center. The summary presented site options, possible program and facility components, cost forecasts, and funding alternatives. The findings were compiled into a report recommending that the alliance pursue the development of a shared wellness and fitness center.

The exploratory committee presented the report to the policy committee. The members then held a joint meeting to share their findings with the boards of their organizations before deciding on the next steps. With the completion of the report, the alliance had fulfilled its original purpose. However, with the approval of their organizations' boards, the leaders used the report as the foundation for renewing their commitments to the affiliation and pursuing the feasibility of developing a shared wellness facility.

—PROCESS #2

The alliance members identified the more defined exploration of the shared wellness facility as their new goal and chose to continue the affiliation without modifying its structure. The leadership, membership, and structure of the affiliation remained unchanged. The leaders and organizational members maintained their original roles, and the alliance continued based on the verbal agreements of the executives to pursue the new goal.

The policy committee engaged an external consultant to conduct a comprehensive feasibility study of the proposed health and wellness project. When the policy committee decided to go forward with the study, each organization made a financial commitment: the college contributed $20,000, the YMCA contributed $1,000, and the hospital agreed to pay the balance of the cost. The hospital took the lead on the payment because it hired specific consultants with expertise in hospital partnerships.

At about this point, the YMCA began to experience some tension around the process. Conducting a feasibility study was time-consuming, but the YMCA's executive recognized that it was a necessary step for the hospital and college. Their organizational decision-making processes were more complex than the YMCA's, and they needed to maintain appropriate accountability with relevant stakeholders in both the private and public sectors. The YMCA, a much smaller community agency, was unaccustomed to this more detailed and deliberate process, and its protracted nature led to some frustration for board and staff.

Members representing the YMCA were empowered to make most decisions in the alliance on behalf of the organization. The board had given its approval to proceed with the project. Therefore, the YMCA did not require extensive study or consideration prior to moving ahead. In contrast, the size and complexity of the other institutions did not permit their representatives similar decision-making authority, and regardless of how appealing the idea of developing a joint wellness facility, they had to meet additional accountability requirements before they could proceed.

The YMCA was committed to the project but wanted to see more progress. The organization was able to temper its concerns by reassessing its role in the alliance. In contrast to its position when it entered the alliance, after 2 years of participation, the YMCA was more stable organizationally. It no longer perceived the affiliation as necessary for its survival. Its reasons for participating had evolved. The YMCA now saw itself as a stronger organizational partner and, as such, chose to continue participating in the affiliation because it believed in the mission of the project and that it was beneficial for the community and the alliance members. Focusing on these ends, the YMCA was able to lessen its frustration with the process and remain involved.

—OUTCOMES #2

The affiliation has resulted in several significant outcomes, although no facility has been built. The alliance completed the feasibility study. The study tested a number of ideas: stakeholder reaction to the partnership, the location, the competition, current use of a fitness facility, and the price for membership. The response was positive, and the study recommended that the process proceed. Fitness competition in the area was minimal, and the public felt good about the ability of these three organizations to provide a credible fitness facility.

Another key outcome of the Shared Wellness Project affiliation was that the member organizations have established a high degree of trust with each other. This trust has resulted in successful spin-off activities among the three organizations to promote health and wellness in new communities. The YMCA has conducted programs at the hospital and the college. The hospital and college also offered some of their programs at the YMCA, and the three are considering the development of a joint venture to create a health and wellness center.

From the YMCA's perspective, the affiliation has been a success. It has benefited the member organizations and the community. The cross-over use of each other's facilities to offer health and wellness programs, for example, can continue regardless of whether the members formally move ahead to develop the joint wellness center.

—REPORTER'S REFLECTIONS AND LESSONS LEARNED

Two key lessons emerged from the YMCA's participation in this alliance. The YMCA learned that it is necessary to both identify the needs and goals of each organization at the beginning of the alliance development process, and refer back to these throughout the course of develop-

ment, especially when trying to resolve challenges. Second, the organization realized how important it is that alliance members not underestimate
the value of this and other activities that focus on the process of developing
trust, which it identified as an essential ingredient in successful alliance
efforts.

PRELIMINARY ANALYSIS:
SOME THOUGHTS ON DEVELOPMENT

Theoretical Perspectives

The Shared Wellness Project was driven largely by the members' desires for improved or expanded services in the area of health and wellness
and the need for economies of scale to make the goal of establishing a new
facility in which to offer these services a viable proposal. These motivations are consistent with the need for strategic enhancement and operational efficiency. The focus on service improvement corresponds with the
basic assumption of the strategic enhancement perspective, as does the
YMCA's initial position that the alliance was necessary for the organization's survival.

The members' goal of increasing capabilities to provide these services
through the joint creation of a new fitness facility corresponds with the
primary tenet of the operational efficiency perspective. Not only did the
partners share the same goal, but also each had unique and critical resources to contribute to the operations of the facility. The YMCA had expertise in administering health and wellness programs and supplied a link
to the resources of the national YMCA.

The hospital and the college offered other resources, including access
to different public and private funding sources, a broader potential consumer base, wider community influence, and a possible site for the facility. Combining the existing resources of the three organizations to
accomplish a mutual goal would create economies of scale for the project
that would not exist if any of the organizations attempted to implement
the project on its own. Moreover, the hospital's emphasis on increasing
cost-effectiveness and accessibility further bolsters the rationale for the
development of the alliance from a perspective of operational efficiency.

Although strategic enhancement and operational efficiency were
shared goals of alliance participation, the YMCA entered the initial alli-

ance with a third motive: to increase its environmental validity. Not only was the executive director of the YMCA new to the position when the alliance began, but the organization was not operating from a position of strength within the institutional community. It had suffered for the past few years from a negative public image that it was hoping to overcome. By participating in the alliance, the YMCA was able to increase its legitimacy with two larger organizations by providing them needed expertise in health and recreational programming. In addition, the alliance offered the YMCA opportunities for greater visibility in the community and contacts with groups not previously accessible to it.

As the YMCA's position in the community improved, the organization's motivation for participation in the alliance changed. Although the organization remained focused on enhancing service delivery to access a wider population (strategic enhancement), it moved from seeking increased environmental validity to social responsibility. Once the YMCA was more secure institutionally, its motivational emphasis shifted away from improving its credibility with other organizations to maximizing benefits for the community. The focus of its primary concern was to further enhance its reputation with its consumers and area residents.

Alliance Model

The choice of the affiliation model was an appropriate one for the purpose of exploring a more formal alliance to further the Shared Wellness Project. A loose connection among the members was all that was necessary to facilitate the process. In the alliance, organizational interdependence was based largely on the exchange of information among members and their constituencies. Tasks focused on data collection, analysis, and presentation and could be readily segregated by organization.

Similarly, the task of conducting programs in other members' facilities did not require additional structural formality or integration. One member provided the facility and the consumers, and the other members contributed the program. This type of resource exchange is characteristic of cooperative alliances such as affiliations.

Even when considerable funding was needed to conduct the feasibility study, the organizations divided the cost based on each organization's ability to pay and the degree to which it would benefit from the study. Furthermore, the study was a one-time task for which each organization contributed an agreed-upon amount of money. The alliance partners did not pool financial resources for ongoing activities or program operations, again reducing the level of formality required to pursue the goal and supporting the choice of an affiliation as the alliance structure.

Finally, the choice to begin the alliance as an affiliation provided the organizational members a forum to work together in a less formal and integrated relationship. It gave the members time to develop a level of trust with each other that would strengthen future and more formal efforts. If the decision is made to share ownership of a new facility, the affiliation will have to transition to a more formal alliance model that is consistent with its members' increased interdependence. Joint fund-raising, not to mention the potential for land sharing and the construction and operation of a building, will necessitate greater integration among members than is accomplished through an affiliation structure. Likewise, the legal and liability issues associated with joint ownership of the facility will require more formal agreements among members. Feasible structural configurations could include a consortium and a joint venture.

Phases of Development

The alliance moved through the assembling and ordering phases of development relatively quickly. Several factors contributed to this progress. First, the member organizations had interlocking directorates. In other words, they had board members in common. The organizations' board members and policy volunteers had firsthand knowledge of the compatibility of each organization's goals and were able to expedite the member identification process. In addition, the initial members of the alliance were the executives of the partner organizations, with an appropriate level of authority to make decisions on behalf of the organizations. Although such high-level participation is not necessary in all affiliations, the tasks associated with pursuing the Shared Wellness Project, in this case, required it. However, even with the involvement of administrative staff and board members, the discrepancy in the complexity of the decision-making systems among the member organizations tested the alliance.

The existing relationship between the hospital and college simplified the "getting to know you" aspect of the assembling phase, although it could have presented a significant challenge for the alliance. With two members already familiar with one another, the YMCA might have had a difficult time establishing its presence as an equal partner in the alliance. Fortunately for the YMCA, its expertise in the area of health and wellness programming made it a desirable partner with resources that the other members needed to achieve the alliance's goal. This expertise helped the

YMCA counterbalance the tension that can occur when a new member is trying to position itself within an already established relationship. This is an important consideration in any strategic alliance, especially as new members are added throughout the alliance's evolution.

The choice of the affiliation model also streamlined the initial assembling and ordering phases. Because the Shared Wellness Project began as an informal and loosely coupled alliance, members did not need to relinquish their autonomy in order to achieve the initial purpose of the alliance: exploring the possibility of the partners working together to create a joint wellness facility. The development of the alliance was aided as well by the fact that its purpose corresponded so closely with each of the member organizations' individual goals, and the costs associated with achieving this purpose were limited, involving mostly staff time.

The risks associated with alliance participation were minimal. The members retained their abilities to preserve organizational autonomy and identity while working to achieve a purpose consistent with each member's organizational goals, and the potential costs to the members associated with these activities reduced its risks. With the organizations less concerned about the possible risks involved in alliance membership, they were able to devote more time and energy to developing trust and supporting the evolution of the alliance.

Because the members had identified the initial alliance structure as an affiliation, no formal agreements or complex systems were needed, and members had fewer issues to negotiate in the ordering phase. Members agreed to share leadership of the alliance and created the committee structure early in the development process. As such, the alliance spent the majority of its time in the performing phase, implementing its tasks. When the final report on these tasks was complete and presented to the policy committee, the purpose of the initial affiliation was achieved.

The findings from the report and the foundation the alliance had established during the previous months supported the decision by the members in the transforming phase to continue the affiliation. The leadership and membership of the affiliation did not change, so the primary tasks of the alliance as it revisited the assembling and ordering phases were to identify the alliance's new purpose, strategies, and tasks. These did not require greater interdependence among the members, and therefore, no modifications to the alliance structure or systems were required. Again, the affiliation was able to move quickly into the performing phase of development. The subject of this phase was exploring the feasibility of developing joint health and wellness programs, possibly in one new facility.

Once the member organizations agree that they have fulfilled their purpose, they will again be faced with a decision in the transforming phase of development as to whether to continue the affiliation with an amended purpose or to end it. If the affiliation continues, it will need to reconsider the core questions in the assembling and ordering phases of development before moving fully to implementation. If the members choose not to renew the affiliation and elect not to create another alliance structure, members will need to consider such transforming questions as "What were the alliance's successes?" "What were the lessons learned?" and "How will the members celebrate each other and their joint efforts?"

Differences in the members' organizational cultures—particularly between the smaller and less structured YMCA and the two larger, more highly structured organizations—surfaced for YMCA representatives as an element of tension within the alliance. This dilemma is characteristic of the conflict between "autonomy and accountability" (Rosenthal & Mizrahi, 1994, p. 119). The essence of this tension is the need to balance the autonomy of member organizations to make decisions and take action with the need to satisfy the specific accountability requirements of the member organizations and their stakeholders.

In this case, the YMCA had a much lower accountability threshold than did the hospital and college. Fortunately, when the YMCA began to get discouraged that the alliance process was overshadowing its progress, the organization's perception of its role in the alliance and, correspondingly, its reasons for participating in the alliance changed. This evolution helped the YMCA's representatives manage a challenge that may have threatened the future of the alliance. When the YMCA began participating in the alliance, it did so with an internal focus, viewing the alliance and the creation of joint wellness programming as necessary for its own organizational survival. Over time, this motivation changed to one that focused more broadly on the merit of the overall goal for the Ann Arbor community and the benefits that incremental successes provided for each member's stakeholders and the community-at-large.

The issue of member power might have been a greater challenge for the alliance given the relative size and community power of its members. Yet inequity in members' power did not surface as a substantial issue for the affiliation members. One explanation for this may be that each of the organizations shared a vision around expanding health and wellness programming for the community that, individually and collectively, they were able to keep at the forefront of their work.

In addition, from the beginning of the alliance, each of the partners was recognized as bringing particular resources to the alliance that it needed to accomplish its purpose. In particular, the YMCA, the seemingly least powerful partner, was considered to have the operational expertise, whereas the hospital and college were seen as having greater access to monetary and other resources. Consequently, the YMCA undertook much of the day-to-day work, whereas the other partners contributed most of the money to support the alliance's activities. In addition, fostering joint leadership and creating a decision-making system through which each member had an equal vote supported the perception and experience of equity among the partners and supported the alliance's success.

Part III

COORDINATION

The Power of Aligning Tasks

When an HSO decides—or is told—that it could better accomplish its own particular goals or objectives by partnering with complementary organizations around some common task or signal event, it chooses to *coordinate.* Coordination allows otherwise autonomous organizations to align their activities to support events or services by implementing common tasks. Federations, associations, and coalitions are examples of alliances in which organizations coordinate specific operational areas.

Coordination requires a modest amount of structural complexity. The integration of staffs or activities is minimal and tied to the accomplishment of specific tasks. Policies and procedures are generally kept relatively informal. Each member organization typically writes and signs a letter of agreement spelling out its commitments to the alliance. Bylaws may be created to outline basic alliance protocols and the rules of membership. Input from legal representatives is suggested in formalizing the coordinated structure and negotiating associated issues.

The focus of coordination is on the ability of member organizations to pursue their individual organizational goals better by arranging their activities with the activities of other compatible organizations (see Figure P3.1). Because achieving organizational purposes and the corresponding goals of the alliance through coordinated activities is the primary objective, the core value here is the ability to align *self-interest with others' interests.*

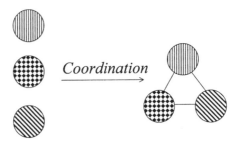

Figure P3.1. Coordination

The loss of autonomy experienced by member organizations through coordination is usually minor, restricted to what is necessary to implement shared tasks, and the risks or level of investment associated with membership are limited. The members remain focused, for the most part, on meeting the goals and objectives of their individual organizations, but they are also aware now of the need to take into consideration the goals and objectives of the other member organizations. So, in coordinated alliances, organizational participation is task-focused while remaining largely organization-based.

Because the emphasis is on getting things done—as opposed to, for example, integrating organizational structures—staff and administrators, and not boards, are typically the primary liaisons between the individual member organizations and the alliance. The organizational integration that occurs takes place around specific tasks and relies most often on member organizations to contribute staff time and services to the effort.

A coordinated alliance may be governed through a formal or informal arrangement, but the full organizational membership is commonly involved in making decisions about the alliance leadership. Unless the alliance bylaws make other provisions, the members typically elect their leaders, often for a period of one to three years.

The systems and processes dealing with alliance decision making and resource integration tend to be task-specific, that is, focused on a particular activity or event. Membership in a coordinated alliance generally requires the contribution of various resources, such as personnel time and supplies. However, it is not uncommon for alliance members to be expected to pay a nominal membership fee, which is used to offset certain costs associated with alliance tasks. Coordinated alliances are not usually integrated to the point of applying jointly for grants. The implementation of activities relies more on the voluntary, or membership-voted, contribution of resources by the alliance members. When members do share substantial levels of resources, the process for allocating such resources is defined formally in the documents governing the alliance.

The size of the membership in a coordinated alliance varies according to the defined tasks but tends to be quite large, because the wish to bring more resources to bear on issues of common concern is generally what brings the members together in the first place. Because coordinated alliances are created to accomplish a specific set of tasks, their duration is task-dependent and, thus, frequently short-term. Interorganizational contact tends to be periodic, occurring only as necessary to implement the specific tasks that the alliance has set for itself; environmental linkages, also tied to specific tasks, will range from few to many.

Chapter 5

FEDERATIONS AND ASSOCIATIONS

Federations and associations are two related forms of coordinated alliances. In these alliances, member organizations centralize common functions such as fund-raising, planning, training, marketing, and/or advocacy. Federations and associations may be thought of as "umbrella" or "parent" bodies that coordinate core tasks for their members. The coordination of these tasks may be carried out more or less formally, with the more formal arrangement often creating an alliance office separate from the member organizations. The following excerpt from the definition of the Jewish Welfare Federation of Detroit illustrates the core concepts of the federation and association model, in this instance, with an emphasis on centralized fund-raising:

> Federation is a partnership of agencies or services seeking financial support jointly through a central campaign. These agencies agree to accept the restraints of some measure of central planning (including budgeting) from the partnership mechanism. Since the association is voluntary, the limitations on central planning and financing extend up to the point which the agency partners are ready to accept. (Avrunin, 1981, pp. 209-210)

In exchange for the benefits derived from centralizing specific tasks, member organizations agree to give up some of their autonomy with respect to the implementation of these tasks. They may be required to pay dues or make an annual contribution to fund the alliance tasks or the alliance office. Members also may be expected to donate staff time and other resources to support its operations. However, member organizations in federations and associations generally remain independent in their ability to carry out their daily activities and maintain individual boards of trustees to oversee their own programs and services.

The federation or association typically sets policies and assumes greater power in areas related to membership responsibilities and the centralized functions. However, like other alliance models, there can be variation in the structure of federations and associations. Depending on how the alliance is ordered, especially when an alliance office exists, the member organizations may have more power to influence the alliance office, or the alliance office may have greater influence over the member organizations. In some structures, the alliance office and the members may share responsibility for certain tasks.

Associations and federations among HSOs are more likely to be organized so that member organizations remain independent and keep more of their identity than in more centrally focused association models, where the alliance office has a greater level of influence over its members. HSO members are apt to share more responsibilities with the alliance office or have more leverage to influence its activities rather than ceding control to the association or federation (Young, Bania, & Bailey, 1996).

Many associations and federations have their roots in the late 19th and early 20th centuries, when the federated fund-raising movement began to gain prominence across the country. One of the first local efforts to centralize fund-raising took place in 1913, when the Federation for Charity and Philanthropy was founded to consolidate philanthropic and charity activities in Cleveland, Ohio (Cutlip, 1965; Romanofsky, 1978). After a long history, the Cleveland Federation evolved into Greater Cleveland's United Way Services and the Federation for Community Planning. Its initial development exemplifies the creation of many federations and associations in the United States and is, therefore, worthy of review here.

The Cleveland Federation for Charity and Philanthropy was founded in response to the financial concerns of local community service organizations and funders. The community service organizations were facing financial difficulties, including budget deficits, and the funders were frustrated with continual pressures to fund these community organizations. According to one of the Federation's earliest publications, its role was to be

> much more than a group of related social organizations working simply for the increase in their own resources or efficiency. The Federation rep-

resent[ed] the plan of a whole community to pool all its resources of time, energy, intelligence, vision, sentiment and inspiration in the attempt to solve the problem of human welfare as it presents itself in the acute forms so familiar . . . in the modern city. (Cleveland Federation for Charity and Philanthropy, 1913, p. 20)

The Federation began with 55 member organizations and was governed by its General Assembly. Each member organization selected two delegates to the General Assembly, which also included ex-officio members from city government and the public schools. The General Assembly was divided into councils with distinct substantive concentrations. Each council had its own budget committee as well as a paid staff liaison with expertise in the content area who coordinated meetings and other activities (Bing, 1938). The General Assembly met annually and oversaw membership and strategic concerns. They also elected the Board of Trustees, who, in turn, appointed staff and committees to implement the Federation's tasks.

The Federation initially coordinated resource procurement and public relations for member organizations. It centralized fund-raising; resource allocation; and publication of materials highlighting its work, the work of its member organizations, and relevant social issues. It also provided ancillary benefits for its members, such as office space leasing opportunities and administrative and planning supports. The Federation offered meeting rooms, a copy machine, bookkeeping services, and the coordination of other financial management functions to its members through the central office (Bing, 1938).

In exchange for the availability of these services, membership in the Federation required organizations to adhere to several criteria. The Federation's membership guidelines placed restrictions on member organizations' individual fund-raising activities to maximize the effectiveness of the central fund-raising campaign. As members, organizations could not seek donations for current expenses from Federation contributors or organize fund-raising events such as bazaars and fairs. They had to consult the Federation about potential fund-raising needs and opportunities and were required to adhere to Federation audit and reporting mandates (Bing, 1938; Federation for Charity and Philanthropy, 1913).

The Federation expanded its mission in 1917 when it merged with the Cleveland Welfare Council and changed its name to the Welfare Federation. The merger was precipitated by two separate, but equally important issues. First, social workers associated with the Federation wanted the organization to extend its activities beyond fund-raising. At the same time, the Welfare Council, which was created in 1914 as a facilitator of community welfare planning, found that it was limited in its activities because it had no budget or paid staff. With this merger, the newly created Welfare Federation sought to address both philanthropic and welfare concerns and broadened its mission to concentrate more actively on research and planning in areas such as health, housing, public assistance, child care, youth crime, and child abuse (Bing, 1938).

In 1919, the Federation created the Community Chest to oversee its local, centralized fund-raising campaign. This program was the precursor to the United Appeal, which began in 1957. The Federation divested its central fund-raising and allocation functions in 1972, creating Greater Cleveland's United Way Services. The Federation reorganized itself and changed its name to the Federation for Community Planning. With United Way Services managing the combined appeal for its members, the Federation for Community Planning continued to focus on planning, research, and the coordination of resources to promote systemic, community-based change.

Today's federations and associations have developed in much the same way as the earliest ones. The following case study describes how a group of organizations in one metropolitan area came together at the request of the local United Way and established an association that offered a range of benefits to all of its members.

Case Study: **Agency Directors Association**
Reporter: **General City YMCA**[1]

—OVERVIEW

The Agency Directors Association is a coordinated effort involving the 30 organizations that receive funding from the United Way in General City. The purposes of the association are to provide a coordinated forum through which agency directors can jointly address critical issues affecting the nonprofit sector, and to serve as a resource for the United Way. The association's membership is diverse and represents the breadth of local section 501(c)(3) agencies supported by the funder. In addition to the General City YMCA, association members include faith-based social service organizations, local service providers, and advocacy organizations focused on individual health and social issues. An advisory council elected by the general membership leads the association.

—PRECONDITIONS

When the General City YMCA hired a new executive director in the early 1990s, the agency was experiencing a financial crisis. It had become so dependent on the local United Way that the survival of more than one of its branch offices, and ultimately the agency, relied on continuation of its annual allocation. To that end, the new executive director targeted the need to strengthen the organization's relationship with its primary funder as a priority.

At about the same time, many nonprofit organizations, and the combined funding campaigns with which they were associated, were just beginning to regain public support following the national controversy surrounding the financial practices of the United Way of America (Glaser, 1994). The United Way scandal had a negative effect on public fund-raising efforts for local organizations and aggravated broader declines in corporate grants and employee contributions to human service organizations that had been occurring over the previous few years. In addition, political activities and corresponding national sentiment were forecasting public policy changes that could have far-reaching implications for the nonprofit sector.

With nonprofit organizations both locally and nationwide concerned about the heightened environmental instability in the sector, the local United Way was making its second attempt at catalyzing the development of an Agency Directors Association. As the convener of the association, the United Way sought to generate interest and leadership for the association among the agencies it funded.

—PROCESS

The United Way requested that the directors of the 30-plus agencies to which it made annual allocations meet to discuss the possibility of forming an alliance. Invited members included the YMCA; several faith-based social service organizations; youth-, family-, and aging-focused agencies; educational and literacy programs; and local service providers and advocacy groups targeting individual health and social issues. The directors of these organizations met with the representatives from the United Way and, after some discussion, agreed to pursue the formation of an association.

Next, the organizations interested in participating in the association met with the United Way at a 2-day retreat, where they identified their organizational priorities and began structuring the alliance. The broad range of organizational missions among the association members surfaced as a challenge for the organizations from the start. As a result, one of the first issues that the members sought to clarify was how working together could be of benefit to them individually, as well as collectively supporting them and the United Way.

In the course of their discussions, the members concluded that in operationalizing the association's mission, they had to address this issue clearly and decisively. To do this, they identified four strategies that, when implemented, would mutually benefit the members of the association as well as their funder. These strategies focused on assessing human service trends, gathering data to address specific human service concerns, encouraging agency management excellence through training and education, and advising the United Way on relevant issues. In addition, the members jointly developed bylaws that supported the association's strategies and outlined the association's mission, leadership, membership guidelines, systems of decision making, and meeting requirements.

The members created an advisory council to serve as the formal leadership for the association and coordinate its activities. The bylaws specified that the association members would biennially elect six members to serve on the advisory council. The association members would also elect the chair and vice-chair of the council, but this would be done annually. The chair of the council would serve as the association chair and represent the association at the United Way's board meetings.

The formal alliance leadership was complemented by strong, informal leadership. Some alliance members were particularly well respected by their peers, often because of their demonstrated capacity to take action and accomplish things. Thus, in spite of the composition of the advisory council, these members continued to have significant influence in shaping the direction and activities of the alliance.

The United Way-funded agencies comprised the membership of the association. The United Way also participated but did not have a voting role. Instead, it assigned a staff liaison to the alliance to support its activities.

Association member agencies were required by the alliance bylaws to pay annual association dues of $50 regardless of organizational size, budget, or funding allocation. Membership dues were used to subsidize association training events and other activities.

Once the association began meeting regularly, it became clear that the degree of involvement among funded agencies varied widely, and the association faced a challenge in determining how to maintain its membership. The majority of the funded agencies were actively involved in the association. However, a number of those eligible for membership either paid their dues but did not participate on a regular basis or did not contribute to the alliance at all. In addition, some of the active member agencies periodically questioned their continued participation at times when the association focused on issues in which they preferred not to engage or in which they did not share an interest.

In an attempt to sustain member investment in the alliance, the association leaders worked with the members to design activities that appealed to a wider range of their interests. For example, the association conducted a benefits survey in which it polled member agencies about their employee benefits and compensation packages. The association summarized the findings and provided its members with a report, which they could use to inform their management decisions. The association began sponsoring quarterly training sessions for members' administrators and staff and emphasized the advantages of having regular opportunities to share information with each other as well as the funder.

With membership in excess of 30 organizations and with the distinct differences in the members' missions, establishing effective decision-making systems was critical for the alliance. The association bylaws stated that a majority vote was required for recommendations to be approved. However, the association developed an informal policy to work toward unanimous support prior to taking action on an issue. Subcommittees were created as necessary to investigate each issue sufficiently to permit informed voting by each member, and the association was not likely to move forward if the issue received only majority support.

Another challenge that the association encountered was how the organizations perceived themselves in relation to each other. Members who did not necessarily define themselves as peers before membership in the alliance now had a greater realization of themselves as both partners and competitors with each other, especially when United Way funding allocations occurred each year. One strategy to address this challenge was illustrated by how the YMCA sought to manage it when the organization's executive served as the chair of the alliance.

In his leadership role, the YMCA's executive worked to keep members focused on the importance of the partnership among the member agencies and the value to all the members of the relationship between the association and the United Way. Member agencies varied in their level of dependence on the funder, but the YMCA's executive stressed the role of the association in supporting the growth of the United Way and the benefits to its members of doing so. The overriding message was that if the association helped the United Way to grow and raise more money, the logical consequence was that there would be more money to distribute among the member agencies.

—OUTCOMES

During the first 5 years of the association, the members engaged in many tasks in accordance with their stated strategies. The association developed a code of ethics as a response to the national United Way leadership controversy and a similar local issue involving the director of one of the association's member agencies. The code was a set of standards aimed at maintaining the integrity of the association's member agencies.

The association sent letters to public officials stating its position on specific legislation and making recommendations on pertinent issues. It sponsored political forums during election years in which invited candidates discussed topics of interest to the nonprofit sector before an audience of community and organizational representatives. It also coordinated quarterly training workshops for the directors and staff of member organizations on topics such as supervisory skills, endowment development, and volunteer management.

Although such tasks are ongoing, in keeping with the association's purpose, much of the more recent work of the alliance has focused on enhancing the efficiency of its member organizations. After several years of association membership, the YMCA became interested in how the member agencies could become more efficient by combining their purchasing power. With the support of the association, the YMCA took the lead in investigating this issue beginning with the purchase of office supplies. It surveyed the members to determine their needs and annual budgets for copy paper and related items. On behalf of the association, the YMCA successfully approached suppliers with the concept of developing a supplier agreement for the association and its members. Following a call for bids, the association negotiated an agreement in which member organizations could purchase copy paper for nearly half of what many of the members were paying per case and could receive a fixed percentage discount on purchases of other office supplies through the contracted supplier.

Participation in the purchasing agreement was not mandatory. However, the association members informally committed to a minimum purchasing level, because the benefit of the agreement was based on the power of quantity purchasing. Despite initial concerns, the concept received significant support, and the supplier and members were satisfied with the outcome. Consequently, the association is trying to negotiate a similar agreement for the purchase or lease of communications equipment such as pagers and cell phones. In addition, the United Way and some of the agency directors are considering consolidating certain functions, such as bookkeeping, to further enhance the efficiency of the funded agencies.

These outcomes largely benefit the individual, organizational members of the association. However, the association also developed a set of communication standards that was designed to support the United Way. In conjunction with these standards, members identify themselves as partners with the United Way and display both the United Way's logo and their own on letterhead and other publications. They provide client-focused stories to the United Way as requested for publicity. They recognize the United Way and its donors in agency communications, participate in the United Way's special events and annual meetings, and actively assist the funder in its annual campaign by providing speakers to support the fund drive and engaging in related efforts. Several of these standards were controversial, and there have been differing levels of buy-in on their implementation. However, as with other association policies, the standards are not mandatory. Each member organization chooses how and when to comply and accepts to a greater or lesser extent that compliance with the protocol is likely monitored by the funder.

—REPORTER'S REFLECTIONS AND LESSONS LEARNED

Although the association does not have specific evaluation criteria to measure its effectiveness, the YMCA views the alliance as a success because of the ongoing, active participation and commitment of the United Way-funded agencies. In addition, it has been particularly beneficial to the organization from a public relations perspective. Finally, involvement in the Agency Directors Association continues to reinforce for the organization that strategic alliances can and do work.

PRELIMINARY ANALYSIS:
SOME THOUGHTS ON DEVELOPMENT

Theoretical Perspectives

The YMCA's involvement in the Agency Directors Association illustrates an important, and often overlooked, characteristic of strategic alliances: The rationale for membership in an alliance can change over time. The YMCA joined the association as a means of strengthening its relationship with the United Way, its primary funder. Although some might consider this action "political," it should not be confused with the domain influence perspective of alliance development under which organizations participate in alliances to increase their power and control. Rather, for the

YMCA, this motivation was congruent with the perspectives of environmental validity and strategic enhancement.

Organizations concerned with environmental validity seek to foster or improve relationships with other organizational stakeholders. For HSOs and other nonprofit organizations, the necessity of securing external funding makes building positive relations with the funding community a constant focus. In the case of the YMCA, this motivation linked with the perspective of strategic enhancement as well. The YMCA's leaders recognized that the survival of several of its branches was dependent on the annual United Way funding allocation. Thus, the organization needed to act where it could to preserve the funding stream, or it would be unable to continue offering its full range of services to the community. The move to preserve the survival of its branches was driven by a need for strategic enhancement. Joining the Agency Directors Association and increasing its environmental validity offered the YMCA an opportunity to do this. By supporting this initiative, which had been convened by the United Way, the YMCA increased its connection and visibility with its primary funder.

The broader context for the development of the alliance further supported the desire for environmental validity as a central motivating factor in the formation of the alliance. This had been the United Way's second attempt to start such a partnership; the first was unsuccessful. When the idea for the alliance was raised, the environmental conditions for the United Way and its member agencies were primed for coordination. They were struggling to regain the public support they had lost as a result of the controversy involving the national United Way.

The local United Way needed a way to bolster its credibility and the legitimacy of its member organizations in the community in order to grow its funding drives. Similarly, many United Way-funded organizations were looking for ways to assist the United Way so that their funding allocations would not be reduced as a result of declining contributions. Once again, the focus was on preserving stakeholder confidence. If the area organizations that contributed to the combined annual appeal did not have faith in the reputation of the local United Way or the organizations it funded, the appeal would suffer, and funding allocations would continue to decrease.

Whereas these factors initially led the YMCA and the other members to join the Agency Directors Association, after several years of membership, the YMCA's primary interest in the association changed. As the local United Way and the association's member organizations regained strong community support, the YMCA became more interested in how interorganizational coordination could create economies of scale for the member organizations, a motive for participation consistent with the perspective of operational efficiency. Thus, the YMCA's rationale for maintaining membership in the alliance differed from the reason it joined the alliance, and these motivations may continue to change over time.

Alliance Model

The structure and systems of the Agency Directors Association are characteristic of a model association. Its members pay dues, which are used to support the association's activities. An association also typically centralizes specific functions for its members, and member organizations retain their autonomy outside the alliance. The Agency Directors Association coordinated training events and public policy efforts and began centralizing purchasing activities and external communications protocols. However, compliance was voluntary, and the extent to which member agencies participated in association activities remained at the discretion of each member organization. Even with respect to joint activities, the member organizations retained their organizational identities. For example, in complying with the established communications standards, alliance members displayed the United Way's logo in conjunction with their own, not in place of it.

The association was less centralized than some HSO associations. It did not create an association office with a core staff to support its activities. Rather, members contributed time and other organizational resources as necessary to accomplish their tasks.

If the primary purpose of the alliance had been information sharing, it might have operated as effectively through cooperation as it did through coordination. However, jointly conducting ongoing activities such as staff training and quantity purchasing created a somewhat more integrated alliance. Because the success of these activities relied on creating economies of scale, organizational commitments also needed to be defined more clearly, thus increasing its formalization. The creation of bylaws and the payment of annual dues provided the basis for this structure without necessitating that the member organizations give up too much of their autonomy. In this way, the member organizations did not have to move to collaboration, a more integrated and formal process, to achieve their goals.

Phases of Development

The local United Way was the alliance convener and began the assembling process. Although in many cases, the alliance convener becomes the formal leader of the partnership, the United Way did not continue as the association leader once the alliance was formalized. In fact, the United Way was not a member of the association but served as an environmental linkage—a stakeholder who supports (and, in this case, directly benefits from) the alliance but does not have official membership status.

The United Way identified the preliminary purpose and membership of the alliance and invited the potential members—the agencies it funded through annual allocations—to a meeting to discuss the possibility of pursuing a partnership. When the organizations agreed to proceed, the United Way convened a 2-day retreat to begin structuring what would become the Agency Directors Association, quickly transitioning the alliance from the assembling to ordering phase of development. One thing that may have eased this transition was the fact that the alliance-building process was being initiated by a funder at the same time that the member organizations were looking for ways to recover from a period of declining revenues.

It was at the 2-day retreat that the alliance formalized its purpose and strategies as well as its membership, leadership, and structural guidelines. It was also during this meeting that the members first identified what would become an ongoing challenge for the association: the diversity of its organizational membership. The primary dimensions of this diversity were in the organizations' differing missions and the ideologies underlying them.

Although some associations or federations are formed around the similar missions of the members (e.g., an association of child care agencies), some, like the Agency Directors Association, are formed under more general auspices. In this case, the common theme uniting the member organizations was the funder, not a mission or programmatic component, resulting in a broader membership with less similar organizational purposes. To coordinate their efforts effectively, the members had to continually reassess how well they were balancing their sometimes divergent goals to manage this tension of "unity and diversity" (Rosenthal & Mizrahi, 1994, p. 121).

During the assembling and ordering phases of development, the members addressed this issue by jointly creating a purpose and strategies for the association that offered clear benefits for each of its member organizations, as well as the United Way. These were defined broadly so that they encompassed the multiple interests of the member organizations and included such things as keeping informed on issues relevant to the nonprofit sector and providing coordinated training for members' administrators and staff.

The association's policy of a rotating leadership team also assisted it in dealing with this issue. The association created a six-member advisory council to lead the alliance. The association membership elected the advisory council members for 2-year terms and elected a new leader of the advisory council each year. Moreover, the association relied heavily on the informal leadership of its most respected organizational members to guide its activities. In this way, many organizational perspectives, not to mention personal styles, were integrated into the leadership of the association.

The issue of membership diversity challenged the association again in the performing phase and threatened the association's ability to sustain its membership. If the association spent too much time focusing on a particular set of issues to please one contingent of organizations (e.g., those interested in health policy), the other organizations might begin to view the costs of membership in the alliance as higher than the benefits and stop participating. Therefore, during this phase, what became most important for the members in managing this challenge was defining their tasks in such a way to support their strategies and bridge their multiple interests.

Once again, the way the alliance was structured and the systems it had put in place helped the alliance as it negotiated these tensions. In particular, the choice of the alliance to work toward unanimous decisions before undertaking a task or taking action on an issue reinforced the importance of each member's voice in the alliance and ultimately contributed to more favorable outcomes. It assured dissenting members that their points of view would be taken seriously and addressed constructively by the group, not simply disregarded by the consensus of the majority. This way, the alliance was not placing the desires of selected members above those of others. In addition, members were given flexibility in determining when and whether they would participate in an association activity (e.g., a training session) or comply with a protocol (e.g., the communications standard developed to support the United Way). Although this approach is often easier to accommodate in a less formal alliance, such as this one, this approach promotes a greater sense of control that may make it easier to continue participating in the alliance. Moreover, it helps members keep perspective on the fact that participation in the alliance does not require them to give up too much autonomy and, thus, may assist them in assessing the benefits commensurately.

Finally, thinking broadly in defining tasks helped the association maximize the benefits of participation for the organizational members. Organizations not as interested in policy education on a particular topic could still benefit from participating in the trainings or the joint purchasing agreement. It is worth noting that the formation of alliances to take advantage of joint purchasing opportunities is increasing among HSOs, and in the nonprofit sector in general. In practical terms, and with few exceptions, given the finite funding available to HSOs, the direct financial benefits to members of such alliances can be well worth alliance participation.

In the performing phase, the association has also been successful in helping members balance coordination and competition. Effective coordination can be threatened when members place priority on their view of others as competitors—in this case, for United Way funding—rather than on the greater rewards of working together. The association has worked to overcome this issue through continued emphasis by leaders (formal and informal) on finding the shared value or goal on which everyone could agree. For example, the YMCA worked to keep all the members focused on how collective support of the United Way would benefit each agency by increasing the pool of money that the funder had to allocate each year. Ultimately, to continue to balance this tension, leaders must keep the members focused on channeling their combined strengths in pursuit of a broader impact for the member organizations and their stakeholders, including their consumers.

NOTE

1. Identifying information was removed from this case at the request of the reporter.

Chapter 6

COALITIONS

As with many of the terms used in this book, the term *coalition* has been used in different ways both in the literature and in practice. Boissevain (1974) defined a coalition broadly as "a temporary alliance of distinct parties for a limited purpose" (p. 171) and described coalitions that varied in the degree to which leadership and decision making were centralized as well as in other characteristics related to goals and membership. Other authors have linked coalitions more specifically with an issue or advocacy focus, the underlying premise being that organizations in coalitions seek to increase their power and influence through the coordinated efforts of diverse organizations or groups (Dluhy, 1990; Gentry, 1987; Rosenthal & Mizrahi, 1994; Winer & Ray, 1994). According to Roberts-DeGennaro (1987), the emphasis of such coalitions on "interactions . . . directed towards purposive change" (p. 66) sets them apart from less formal alliance models.

In short, a coalition is defined as an alliance through which organizations come together to address a commonly agreed-upon political or social change goal while largely retaining their organizational autonomy. Coalitions may coordinate other activities to benefit their membership, but the primary focus remains on the political or social change goal.

Coalition building among HSOs and other community organizations is considered a useful strategy of organizing (Checkoway, 1987; Fisher & Karger, 1997; Haynes & Mickelson, 1997; Kahn, 1991), and it has a strong history. Coalitions were increasingly used during the civil rights and women's movements in the 1960s and into the early 1970s, gaining prominence as a way to mobilize organizations again in the early 1980s in response to dramatic cutbacks in federal funding for social services. Similarly, coalition building remains a popular interorganizational strategy as funders are calling for coalition-based responses to change service delivery systems and community organizations are trying to get the voices of their consumers heard in the policy debates around welfare reform and other issues.

Coalitions are usually governed by some form of written agreement, such as memoranda of understanding among members, although these agreements may only generally define how the goal will be achieved, what each member's role will be, and/or what resources the members will commit to the process. Depending on its relative integration and formalization, a coalition may have a central staff to coordinate its activities, or it may rely on the donation of staff time and other resources from its member organizations.

Coalitions typically are defined as temporary alliances because of their specific issue focus. However, this does not necessarily mean that coalitions address only short-term issues. Given the pervasiveness of many of the issues that HSOs work to address, ongoing coalitions may, in fact, appear to be more permanent than temporary.

Advice of legal counsel is suggested for organizations entering into or participating in coalitions. With such counsel, member organizations can ensure that the political or social change focus of the coalition and its corresponding activities does not compromise the organization's tax-exempt status or its funding.

People First! provides one example of how a coalition operates. Every other year, in conjunction with the biennial sessions of the Texas legislature, a coalition of 30 statewide organizations and groups representing HSOs came together in Austin to develop the legislative agenda for the People First! coalition.

The coalition was first formed in response to attempts by some Texas legislators to have individual groups representing separate human service contingencies compete with each other for limited state funding rather than expanding funding for human services and health care. However, human service advocates recognized that many of their agencies served the same clients. Decreasing funding in one essential area of need and increasing funding in a different area would still leave their clients struggling against an economic and social status quo.

The primary message of People First! was that the Texas legislature should first fund programs that helped people before funding all other state services and interests. Members of the coalition shared their individual legislative goals and developed a unified platform that was distributed widely across the state to their local members. This process allowed the members of the coalition to become well versed in each other's issues and created a unified platform for addressing the needs of mutual clients.

Members of the coalition met before the legislature convened to identify the legislative agendas of its individual member organizations. The coalition supported the joint funding priorities of the member organizations, building the common agenda for providing sufficient resources for people programs (as opposed to highway or other initiatives). This, then, became the coalition's legislative platform or priority list.

Special People First! lobbying days were planned by the constituent members of each of the organizations that comprised the coalition. Members of the People First! coalition also met with the elected representatives of their legislative districts to discuss their advocacy goals for the legislative session. During the session, local member organizations, acting in response to information provided by the state coalition members, organized telephone advocacy, wrote letters to the editor, and made presentations to educate the general public about the health and human needs of the state.

Members of the coalition donated staff time and resources, meeting space, and printing and distribution of written fact sheets and legislative platforms. Each member was responsible for alerting its own constituencies across the state as to the status of various legislative initiatives and budget appropriations.

The coalition elected officers for each session who were responsible for chairing meetings; getting meeting minutes and announcements distributed; and coordinating legislative advocacy efforts, such as testifying at committee hearings and monitoring the status of bills filed. Although all members agreed to promote the agenda of the coalition, they were still free to promote the agendas of their individual organizations as well.

The People First! coalition represents a relatively informal alliance focused on political and social change through advocacy efforts directed specifically at the Texas state legislature. The following case study provides a more comprehensive examination of a somewhat more formal social change coalition with a broader and more ongoing focus. The case of the Coalition to Monitor Medicare Managed Care illustrates the coalition formation process and highlights some of its challenges and opportunities.

Case Study: **Coalition to Monitor Medicare Managed Care**
Reporter: **Western Reserve Area Agency on Aging**

—OVERVIEW

In mid-1996, the Western Reserve Area Agency on Aging (WRAAA) in Cleveland, Ohio, began a process to establish the Coalition to Monitor Medicare Managed Care. The purpose of the alliance was to educate older people about Medicare managed care benefits and to advocate on behalf of Medicare beneficiaries in a five-county region in northeast Ohio through broad-based coordination. WRAAA convened the coalition and serves as the lead organization. The coalition has 27 organizational members that represent older people as well as the medical, legal, social service, provider, and religious communities. The coalition operates a speakers bureau; issues educational materials concerning Medicare managed care; participates in public policy education; and provides, through a contract with the regional Long Term Care Ombudsman (LTCO), individual assistance with benefit questions, complaints, and appeals.

—PRECONDITIONS

In early 1996, a long-time social advocate in northeast Ohio grew concerned about the impact of managed care on the health care services available to older citizens. Several celebratory events in her life had refocused her attention on the impact of advocacy in promoting social change and the need to protect patients' rights in the managed care process. Her personal and professional reflections, coupled with a rich history as a member of human service alliances, led her to conceive the idea of creating an alliance to ensure that Medicare managed care beneficiaries got safe, timely, and quality care.

At the time, she was a member of the Board of Trustees for WRAAA, a private, nonprofit organization designated by the state of Ohio to respond to the needs of older citizens in a five-county region through advocacy, planning, and program administration. She viewed the organization as having an important role to play in forming an alliance to monitor Medicare managed care. WRAAA had a history of alliance participation, and the proposed goal corresponded with the organization's mission to advocate on behalf of older people.

The board member also perceived the issue to be timely. In the mid-1990s, amid the political debate on how to contain spending and reduce the federal budget deficit, Medicare reform was receiving considerable attention. Medicare spending was projected to more than double in the subsequent decade, and forecasts of Medicare's hospital insurance trust fund predicted that it would run out of money by 2002. One reform proposal being considered was expanding the managed care options available to Medicare beneficiaries with the anticipation that managed care programs would help contain health care spending increases.

In 1995, approximately 9% of Medicare beneficiaries nationwide were enrolled in managed care plans. Unlike traditional fee-for-service Medicare recipients, these consumers received coverage for preventive health and other services, such as regular examinations and prescription drugs. However, concerns about participation in managed care centered on the limits placed on individuals regarding choosing medical providers, the quality of care, patients' rights around treatment given the need for pre-approval before receiving many specialty services, and the capacity of these insurers to enroll more consumers.

In northeast Ohio, there were 348,000 Medicare beneficiaries in WRAAA's five-county region. Enrollment in Medicare managed care plans was expanding rapidly. In one year, enrollment grew from 14% to 22%. With increasing enrollment in Medicare managed care, the WRAAA board member believed that interest in the issue of monitoring Medicare managed care would be shared by many other organizations in the area. She saw the ongoing focus on Medicare reform and Medicare managed care options as critical factors in organizing the effort to advocate on behalf of the area's Medicare consumers. Moreover, she believed that creating an inter-organizational partnership would bring greater legitimacy and power to the work.

—PROCESS

The WRAAA board member presented the idea of forming an alliance to WRAAA's executive director. Once she obtained his support, she raised the issue with the agency's board. The original proposal for the alliance was to bring together a small group of organizations to advocate on behalf of the Medicare beneficiaries in WRAAA's five-county service region. The board, concerned about the impact of managed care on Medicare recipients, unanimously approved the concept.

WRAAA was the alliance convener and has continued to serve as its organizational leader. The Coalition to Monitor Medicare Managed Care was established to operate as a project of WRAAA, and the WRAAA board member who originally conceived the alliance has served as its chair from the start.

The first step for WRAAA in creating the alliance was to gain support from several key organizations that it felt would be instrumental in the planning process. To this end, WRAAA's executive director and the initiat-

ing board member met with the president of a large medical service organization to discuss the Medicare managed care issue and the organization's
possible interest in participating in the alliance. The goal of this conversation was to begin solidifying the potential membership, which would
include organizations representing the consumer, medical, legal, and provider communities, as well as organizations with strong volunteer bases.

The WRAAA legal counsel assisted in getting support from a major
community legal organization that joined the coalition, and WRAAA met
with the local LTCO. WRAAA asked LTCO to provide staff support for the
coalition project and a direct service component of individualized information, assistance, and advocacy for older people negotiating Medicare managed care.

WRAAA and LTCO had an existing relationship. WRAAA, the state
designee for the administration of the programs funded through the Older
Americans Act in a five-county region in northeast Ohio, served as the local
federal funding agent for the Act's ombudsman services. However, because
these requests represented a major organizational commitment of staff resources and an expansion of LTCO's Medicare advocacy to include all coverage issues (not just those involving long-term care), LTCO's board of
trustees underwent a process to decide and approve the proposed level of
coalition participation.

LTCO, a private, nonprofit agency designated by the Ohio Department
of Aging, was mandated by law to provide information, counseling related
to complaints, and advocacy for consumers of long-term care services. In
Ohio, ombudsman work included the whole continuum of long-term care,
from skilled nursing facilities to home- and community-based services.
LTCO had developed and received funding for a Medicare Advocacy Project assisting consumers with benefits and appeals. Thus, working with the
coalition was a logical extension of that program. LTCO was also a trusted
advocate in the community with no conflict of interest. The long-term
thinking was that, eventually, LTCO would be able to absorb this function
on a regular basis.

Each of these organizations helped to identify prospective alliance
members. One of the primary criteria for selection was the knowledge
and influence base each organization could bring to the alliance effort.
As discussion among the organizations continued, the potential membership grew. Once a strong group of possible members was identified, the
WRAAA board sent letters to these organizations introducing the alliance
and inviting them to participate.

The coalition met monthly as the alliance was being formalized. The
first meetings focused on creating a shared understanding of the alliance
and crafting the alliance's mission and goal statements. The coalition's
mission was to advocate on behalf of Medicare beneficiaries and work to

ensure that managed care organizations were accountable to their consumers and that they operated in the public interest. Its goals supported this mission, and both were approved at the second coalition meeting. Next, the members began detailing the tasks that would have to be accomplished to achieve these goals.

The initial coalition meetings also included discussion about membership guidelines, and several key issues were raised. First, members agreed that it was important to ensure representation from across the five-county region covered by the alliance. Second, the coalition considered how members would balance the multiple, and often competing, demands of representing themselves, their organizations, and their professions as members of the alliance. The members agreed that this issue could be managed if they continually emphasized that, when acting as part of the coalition, they were a voice for the consumers' interests.

Because of the advocacy role the alliance intended to serve, another issue that the members had to address was the potential for conflicts of interest. Each organizational member except LTCO could identify at least some level of conflict between its work and its participation in the coalition because of the pervasive nature of managed care. However, rather than abandoning the coalition, members elected to acknowledge that potential conflicts of interest existed and to set some membership guidelines to minimize them. For example, the members agreed that conflicts of interest for managed care organizations would be too great to allow them to become coalition members.

The coalition established five task forces to carry out the work of the alliance. These task forces corresponded with the coalition's goals and focused on community education, informed choice, data collection and analysis, public policy, and complaints and appeals. Each member was asked to participate on at least one coalition task force. The task forces were created to engage in activities around their focal areas with a relatively high degree of independence. Coalition staff were assigned by WRAAA and LTCO to provide support for meetings and activities associated with their work. All recommendations and decisions from the task forces had to be brought to the full coalition for approval before implementation on behalf of the coalition.

The decision to require full coalition approval before implementing task force recommendations arose from a public policy issue that both challenged the coalition early and briefly threatened its cohesiveness. After the coalition had approved its public policy agenda, the public policy task force identified a bill then before the state legislature that fit with its agenda. The task force sent letters of support for the bill to state legislators. After the letters were sent, one of the coalition's member organizations expressed anger about the action.

The coalition leader facilitated the management of this potentially divisive issue by engaging the members in a dialogue that first examined the issue in the context of the individual members' competing interests and then considered those interests in relation to the primary goal of the coalition. The members ceded priority to the coalition's goal but agreed that before any legislation was endorsed in the future, the recommendation would be reviewed and approved by the coalition as a whole. This decision became less relevant when the coalition received funding for its activities that permitted the coalition to engage in public policy education but did not allow for the endorsement of specific legislation.

Several months into the process, the coalition chose to formalize its membership through written agreements. The coalition membership agreement required organizations to support the coalition's mission, goals, and public policy agenda. In addition, the agreement stipulated that member organizations commit to respond in a timely manner when issues were raised, disseminate coalition information, and contribute volunteers and other resources as considered appropriate by the member organization. Initially, 17 organizations formalized their memberships. New members have continued to join the coalition, some requesting membership and others being invited because of the consumer and other resource bases they offered. Alliance membership now totals 27.

The process of finalizing the purpose, strategies, and structure of the coalition took 6 months. Once this work was completed, the members began concentrating on the need for funding to sustain their work. WRAAA and LTCO assigned staff to work with the coalition from the outset. WRAAA had accessed Title III-F money (from the Older Americans Act) slated for consumer education, and LTCO, funded under the same act, contributed as well to initiate coalition activities. After several months, WRAAA became concerned that the staff assigned to work with the coalition were being required to devote too much time to the alliance, so the organization hired a part-time staff person to coordinate daily activities. One key aspect of the job was to write funding proposals to secure additional resources to staff the task forces of the coalition.

Securing funding to supplement the allocation from the Older Americans Act became a priority, so WRAAA and LTCO contributed staff time and other resources to the coalition until such funding was obtained. Because of the innovative and timely nature of the project, the coalition approached local and national foundations about their interest in funding its work. In the spring of 1998, two local foundations funded the coalition for more than $465,000 over 3 years. The coalition used money from the grants to hire a full-time project manager and a part-time assistant at WRAAA to staff the task forces and coordinate alliance activities. The grants also allowed LTCO to hire additional employees and cross-train all its staff to provide individual counseling and assistance in complaint and appeal resolution to Medicare beneficiaries with concerns about managed care. Additionally, the funding helped hire a consultant to analyze public policy initiatives at the state level.

The coalition is planning beyond the 3-year foundation funding cycle. Its goal is that coalition activities may be continued through appropriate language and funding in the reauthorization of the Older Americans Act or through state funding.

—OUTCOMES

One of the coalition's core activities was consumer education. However, one of its implicit objectives was to avoid duplication of existing information and services available to Medicare beneficiaries. Therefore, the community education task force began its work by identifying gaps in the existing literature about Medicare HMOs that was available to consumers. Many of the publications focused on how to pick an HMO but did not help Medicare beneficiaries determine whether HMOs were the best choice for their needs. In response, through the community education committee, the coalition developed numerous publications to address the information gaps.

To assist Medicare consumers who believed they were required to select a Medicare managed care service plan, the alliance created an information sheet to clarify that the election was a choice, but that maintaining traditional Medicare coverage was also an option. The coalition also published and distributed 20,000 copies of a six-page brochure to assist consumers in deciding which choice was best for them. Other information sheets explained the differences between appeals and grievances, a significant distinction when challenging HMO decisions, and described how to initiate an expedited appeal.

In addition, the community education committee created a speakers bureau to educate the community about Medicare managed care and related issues. By the end of the first year of funding, the coalition trained 30 volunteer speakers from member organizations. These speakers gave 125 presentations, reaching about 7,500 individuals. In 1998, LTCO provided 2,045 hours of service (complaints, appeals, information, training, community education, advocacy, and ongoing work with the coalition and its task forces) to 3,703 individuals. Coalition members met with all of the 10 Medicare HMOs to discuss systemic issues, made presentations to statewide and national conferences, and participated in a Medicare Payment Advisory Commission consumers panel.

The public policy committee created a public policy agenda to focus the advocacy efforts of the coalition. The agenda emphasized the importance of choice for consumers enrolled in Medicare plans and specified elements of quality, communication between managed care organizations and consumers, due process, and oversight that it believed consumers have the right to expect. The details of the agenda guided the coalition's education and advocacy efforts, although, as noted earlier, requirements of current funding do not allow the coalition to endorse specific legislation relating to these issues.

The coalition has established evaluation benchmarks for its activities that it monitors on a regular basis. These criteria relate to services delivered and examine such indicators as the number of people being reached through the coalition's activities. Direct service data are tracked and analyzed to identify consumer problems. LTCO is also involved in an ongoing formative evaluation of the direct service component and is developing consumer outcome measures. The data gathered are analyzed to improve the activities, and they are reported to the funders. Although the coalition also tracks its membership numbers, it does not have formal evaluation criteria to assess the coalition process specifically.

—REPORTER'S REFLECTIONS AND LESSONS LEARNED

Overall, WRAAA learned several key lessons from its work with this alliance. First, the agency has found that a coalition can work, although attention needs to be paid to what the individual members can contribute to the accomplishment of its mission. Second, in developing and maintaining a successful coalition, there is no substitute for a timely issue. And, finally, committed and supportive staff are important resources in making an alliance work.

PRELIMINARY ANALYSIS:
SOME THOUGHTS ON DEVELOPMENT

Theoretical Perspectives

A number of motives for alliance participation are readily apparent in this case. They include social responsibility, strategic enhancement, environmental validity, and domain influence. The coalition was formed to address a timely issue in an area where consumers' interests needed more protection than is currently built into law. For most organizational members, educating and advocating for Medicare beneficiaries about managed care was not seen as tied directly to their individual organizational missions. So, by participating in the coalition, these organizations were responding to the larger social concerns raised by the emerging Medicare managed care market. From this perspective, they were motivated by social responsibility.

LTCO expanded its mission to allow it to provide services on behalf of the coalition. However, a driving force behind this action was its desire to meet the needs of a wider group of consumers than it had previously served, again reflecting the social responsibility perspective by responding to the needs of the public, and specifically, Medicare managed care consumers. Strategic enhancement was also an aspect of LTCO's decision. Changing its mission enabled the organization to contract with WRAAA and the coalition to provide these expanded services to Medicare managed care recipients and thus broadened the range of services LTCO could offer. In short, LTCO was able to take advantage of a service niche by delivering services that no other organization was providing. In this way, the organization improved its strategic position in a competitive service delivery arena. LTCO's desire for strategic enhancement and improvement of its competitive position was further supported by the alliance's long-term goals to have LTCO permanently absorb the consumer advocacy services and to secure ongoing funding for these services through changes in federal or state authorizations.

WRAAA saw its mission as advocating on behalf of older people. Consumer advocacy around concerns of Medicare managed care recipients certainly fit with that organizational purpose. In much the same way that LTCO did, WRAAA created a unique service role for itself by coordinating the alliance as one of its organizational projects. In doing so, it was both supporting more positive interactions between itself and other organizational stakeholders around issues of concern to older people and enhancing its credibility among funders for taking the lead in such an initiative. In this respect, WRAAA might be seen as operating from the standpoint of increasing its environmental validity.

From the domain influence perspective, the organizations were aware that through participation in the alliance, they could increase the strength they had to advocate for their consumers' interests. Because the overriding purpose of the alliance was to advocate for Medicare managed care consumers, the member organizations were motivated by the desire for greater power to be more effective in accomplishing this goal.

The Coalition to Monitor Medicare Managed Care was formed, in part, so that the alliance could be a stronger voice in raising awareness about the issue of Medicare managed care than any one organization could be alone. The coalition's broad-based membership, representative of five counties and multiple disciplines, increased the resources available to address the relevant issues. The alliance was able to capitalize on the involvement and expertise of organizations from the legal, medical, social service, and faith-based communities to have more impact in the arena of Medicare managed care. Through its organizational membership, the alliance had linkages to an even broader range of stakeholders, further increasing its strength. With these resources, the coalition was positioned to be a more powerful force in educating the community and influencing the Medicare managed care environment in its five-county service area and beyond.

Alliance Model

The choice of the coalition model for this alliance was appropriate, most obviously because of its advocacy focus. The coalition had initially considered itself a consortium, but changed its name early in its development. The name change did not reflect a modification in the alliance structure but was chosen because "the coalition" sounded more appropriate to the members than "the consortium." As it turned out, the choice was also a more accurate one to describe the type of alliance the members had formed. In particular, it emphasized the social and political agenda that the alliance wanted to affect.

The alliance structure was relatively informal, and organizational integration was fairly low, consistent with the coordination process typical of coalitions. Participation in the coalition required that organizations sign written membership agreements. These agreements, with the exception of the contract with LTCO, were broad and did not pose much risk to the members. They focused more on documenting the members' shared agreement with the coalition's purpose and policy agenda than on strictly defining how the coalition would operate or what roles and responsibilities each organization would have in implementing the alliance's tasks. In fact, even where the agreements specified members' commitments to the alliance, they did so by stipulating that members would be responsible for specific tasks, such as disseminating information and contributing volunteers and other resources as appropriate. As such, the relationship of the members to the alliance was one in which members did not give up much autonomy to participate.

Similarly, the coalition's resources were not highly integrated. Members contributed staff time and other resources to the coalition on an as-needed and task-specific basis. With the exception of some of the work done by WRAAA and LTCO, members contributed these resources to the alliance in kind.

LTCO's relationship with the alliance was somewhat more complex than that of the other members. LTCO was a member of the alliance with a contract to provide direct services to consumers on behalf of the coalition. The contract increased the formality of LTCO's connection with the alliance, yet remained consistent with the coalition model. The specifics of every coalition depend on the unique circumstances of the alliance and its members. As such, considerable variation can be seen in the definition of coalition structures. Overall, the Coalition to Monitor Medicare Managed Care was more a means of coordinating the members' separate activities than a mechanism for collaborating through jointly determined strategies to achieve a new, collective purpose, once again supporting its classification as a coalition.

Phases of Development

One of WRAAA's board members was the "issue champion" who provided the momentum for the creation of the coalition. She acted as the individual leader of the alliance representing WRAAA, which served as the organizational leader. When the decision to proceed with the alliance was made by WRAAA, the alliance was established as an organizational project, linking it directly to the services provided by the organization, and further defining WRAAA as its formal leader. Therefore, from the beginning, the leadership of the alliance was centralized at WRAAA, and that organization largely directed its development.

WRAAA defined the issue, generated support within the organization, and invited key stakeholders to come together in the alliance. However, from the earliest stages of the assembling phase, WRAAA worked to secure the participation of other organizations in this process. The trustee and executive director of the alliance personally visited a core group of organizations to secure its commitment to developing the alliance before proceeding. In identifying these organizations, WRAAA selectively identified a legal organization, a medical organization, and an advocacy organization working with related issues. These organizations were representative of the kinds of organizations the alliance hoped to have participating, and each had a strong reputation in the community that would provide more influence in its work.

It was this core group of organizations, not WRAAA alone, that identified the larger group of organizations invited to be members of the alliance. These potential members were chosen because of the resources they could bring to the alliance, including a wide range of perspectives on the target issue. Focusing on the inclusion of diverse organizational interests is one of the central tasks of coalition building.

WRAAA worked with the alliance members, particularly in the first few meetings, to collectively define the parameters of alliance membership and its purpose, strategies, tasks, and structure. One of the issues that the alliance confronted at this point was negotiating the tension of "mixed loyalties" (Rosenthal & Mizrahi, 1994, p. 119). The coalition leader had to help members clarify how they could balance the sometimes competing agendas that they brought to the alliance. In fact, the coalition members openly discussed this issue in early meetings. They acknowledged that, at times, each of them would likely be faced with a conflict concerning how to best manage the multiple demands that were present as they tried to represent the priorities of their organizations, their professions, and their consumers, not to mention their own individual interests. They resolved the issue by agreeing on the need to keep the consumers' interests primary in all coalition activities.

From the time the first alliance meeting was convened, the assembling and ordering phases took about 6 months. Once the alliance entered the performing phase, it relied primarily on its task forces to coordinate its activities. These task forces had a relatively high degree of authority to engage in activities on behalf of the coalition. However, this level of authority created a potentially serious challenge to the coalition when the public policy task force endorsed a piece of state legislation that some coalition members did not support. In negotiating a response to this issue, the coalition returned to the ordering phase of development and modified its decision-making systems. From that point on, all legislative endorsements would be brought to the full coalition for approval before the public policy task force took action on them.

Initially, in the performing phase, funding and supervision for staff to support the task forces came from WRAAA and LTCO. However, in 1998, the coalition received grant funding totaling more than $465,000 for a 3-year period to implement its work.

Although not always characteristic of this type of alliance, many coalitions receive significant sources of revenue. In fact, funders are often mandating coalitions to implement specific initiatives that focus on changing the way services are delivered to consumers and emphasizing social reform. Yet this sharing of substantial financial resources requires that coalitions establish more interdependent systems of resource allocation, and possibly more formal governance policies, than were characteristic of previous social change coalitions. Depending on how they are established, in some cases, these coalitions end up looking a lot like consortia, a type of collaborative alliance, as opposed to a coordinated one.

Because the Coalition to Monitor Medicare Managed Care was established as a project of WRAAA, the organization served as the fiscal agent for the coalition. Thus, WRAAA hired staff and contracted with LTCO to further support the coalition's efforts. Although this increased the formality and interdependence of the relationship between these two organizations, it did not significantly affect their relationships with the rest of the coalition members.

The funding awards presented another developmental challenge for the coalition. To comply with the guidelines of the new funding, the coalition had to change its public policy focus from coalition-based legislative action to public policy education.

Organizing activities around the need for public policy education is a common strategy among coalitions and other alliances engaging in activities directed at political or social change. Some advocacy activities, such as lobbying legislators and endorsing specific legislation, may jeopardize the coalition's funding or threaten the tax-exempt status of the member organizations. Strict attention needs to be paid to this issue at the coalition level as well as the organizational level to ensure that coalition membership does not adversely affect individual organizations or the alliance.

The coalition leader attributed a large part of the success of the coalition to the timeliness of the issue. Organizations were interested and wanted to actively participate even before outside funding was secured. However, the parameters of membership had to be defined clearly in the ordering phase to reduce conflicts of interest that may have threatened the viability and effectiveness of the coalition. The decision to exclude managed care organizations from possible membership was a critical one. It eliminated specific conflicts of interest but also narrowed the avenues available to the alliance for influencing the managed care services provided to the Medicare beneficiaries who enrolled in such programs.

Part IV

COLLABORATION

United by a Common Strategy

Organizations may feel the need to go beyond coordinating their operations around a certain event or practical goal; they may want to develop a joint strategy or common set of strategies for working collectively toward a shared purpose. Consortia, networks, and joint ventures are prevalent models of *collaboration,* the third process on the continuum of strategic alliances.

In a collaborative arrangement, member organizations develop a formal plan for working together on a regular basis. These relationships are typically defined through memoranda of understanding, contracts, or other formal agreements. Bylaws and written protocols govern the scope of work and outline alliance systems such as governance and resource allocation because when organizations collaborate, they commonly integrate a larger proportion of their resources than do less formal alliances formed through cooperation or coordination. In this area of the continuum, these pooled resources more frequently include funding, and organizations in collaborative arrangements often share the work of resource procurement and distribution. Collaborative alliances are often integrated to the point that a separate entity—which may or may not be legally defined or separately incorporated—is formed to carry out the activities of the alliance (see Figure P4.1).

In a collaborative alliance, the member organizations must go beyond respecting one another's differences and learn to manage them effectively and to build consensus around goals and actions that must be taken as a group. The

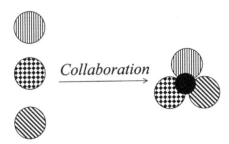

Figure P4.1. Collaboration

members of such an alliance must acknowledge their interdependence and support one another's success in achieving the alliance's goals and building their own organizational effectiveness. The core value for participation in collaborative alliances is *self-interests with other interests* and focuses on the ability to give the interests of fellow members and the interests of one's own organization equal emphasis.

The purpose and strategies in collaboration are alliance based. They are generated collectively and focus on the whole domain in which the partners operate rather than on the isolated issues affecting each of the individual organizations. Because the collaborative alliance's purpose and strategies are grounded in the recognition of the need for interdependence in order to achieve individual organizational effectiveness as well as broader alliance goals, specific tasks are undertaken in an integrated manner rather than being the sole responsibility of individual organizations. Although individual organizations may retain considerable autonomy in their activities outside the scope of the alliance, the collaborative body is ultimately responsible for the oversight of tasks in pursuit of the shared goal and may have significant influence in how they are implemented.

The alliance may be small, with as few as two organizational members and tightly focused, or large and comprehensive, but by definition, a collaborative alliance is usually of ongoing or long-term duration. Because of the relatively high degree of structural complexity found in collaborative alliances, organizational membership will need to include not only staff and administrators but board members, and interorganizational contact will be much more frequent than in less formal alliances. For the same reason, environmental linkages need to be broad-based.

The governance of the collaborative alliance must be representative of its membership, with member organizations sitting on the governing body itself. Alliance policies determine whether these representatives are board, administrators, staff, or consumers of the member organizations. Similarly, alliance systems prescribe the extent to which the governing body assumes liability for alliance activities.

Administrative leadership can be centered in a convening organization, the new collaborative entity, or in some other shared arrangement. In more formal collaborative alliances, even the staffing function of the alliance may be centralized. In these cases, the alliance, and not the individual member organizations, employs and oversees the personnel who perform the tasks of the alliance.

Because decision making is integrated in collaborative alliances, some of the member organizations may be required to alter systems or provisions specific to their organization, such as human resource or management information systems, to comply with alliancewide protocols. Membership in a collaborative alliance also requires a moderately high investment of resources from the partners and carries a corresponding risk. Prospective members should realize that they are going to lose a moderate degree of autonomy, but this is necessary if the alliance's purpose is going to be accomplished through the creation of this common structure and new systems through which the alliance's work is done.

In other words, the collaborative relationship requires more complex and interconnected relationships than exist among cooperating or coordinating organizations. For this reason—coupled with the moderately high degree of structural integration and formality of policies and procedures involved—specialized legal advice should be sought in establishing a collaborative alliance.

Chapter 7

CONSORTIA

A *consortium* is an alliance of organizations that identifies with a particular community or interest domain and wherein member organizations provide their resources collectively to achieve common, often long-term, goals within that domain. Organizations in consortia come together to address an issue or issues that none could address alone, and this alliance type has been described as functioning "as a semiofficial organization of organizations" (Winer & Ray, 1994, p. 23) through which to engage in these efforts.

A consortium provides its members with a means of achieving their common goals through the use of integrated strategies. Consortium members typically collaborate on a shared goal or project, and the consortium is defined by the sum of its parts. That is, a consortium is not usually created to be a legally recognized entity, but rather exists as a formal agreement among a group of organizations to combine its resources for a project that is beyond the members' individual capabilities.

One organization typically serves as the convener, and a core staff (paid by the project or contributed in-kind by its members) administers the joint efforts. Formal agreements, including bylaws and contracts, usually govern interorganizational participation, although organizational members continue to retain their autonomy with regard to matters outside the scope of the alliance.

The alliance is composed of community or domain stakeholders: service providers; agencies or groups; and, sometimes, consumers. In a consortium, members have an active role in governance, including decision and policymaking, which they normally exercise through a central office (or organizing committee) and involvement with one another on consortiumwide issues. Additionally, although the lead agency often retains significant control over the resources and actions of the consortium, it must also actively facilitate the inclusion of all consortium members in these processes. As a result, the leaders in many consortia may have less control over the resources and actions of the alliance members than in cooperative or coordinated alliance models.

Consortia frequently are formed to decrease fragmentation of services in a particular service delivery area or to collaborate on a project that requires the commitment of substantial resources by multiple organizations. Consortia may be created in response to a concern identified by one or more organizations in the community or interest domain, or they may be mandated as a condition of funding.

The Healthy Family/Healthy Start (HF/HS) consortium in Cleveland, Ohio, provides an example of how a public-private service consortium can develop. The HF/HS consortium was convened in 1991 by the Cleveland Department of Public Health (CDPH) in response to a request for proposals from the U.S. Department of Health and Human Services. The development of a community-based consortium was a requirement for federal funding, as was its purpose: to reduce infant mortality and improve health outcomes for women and children by taking a comprehensive approach to services. The rationale for mandating the consortium approach was to stimulate greater innovation and participation in designing and implementing service delivery programs to address the underlying needs of the women and children in local communities.

In creating the alliance, CDPH took a comprehensive view of infant mortality reduction as an interest domain. Thus, the consortium was composed of member organizations that shared concerns in this domain. The members represented hospitals and other health providers, state and local government, social service agencies, educational institutions, businesses, faith-based organizations, and community groups. CDPH has served as the consortium leader from the beginning, and the consortium has continued to establish environmental linkages with other organizations that support its work. Examples of contributions made by these linkages include meeting space; program referrals; car seats, diapers, and other items needed by families; and publicity regarding HF/HS programs and services.

The consortium identified various strategies to achieve its purpose. These strategies depended on interorganizational collaboration and community involvement to implement the HF/HS project effectively, and they included (a) providing community outreach to women and their families to link them with needed medical and other support services, (b) integrating health and social services to improve service delivery to consumers, (c) educating the public to raise awareness about the program and the risk factors associated with infant mortality, and (d) organizing neighborhood councils to promote grassroots involvement in activities to reduce infant mortality. Consortium members developed specific tasks to accomplish these strategies as well.

The HF/HS consortium's purpose, strategies, leadership, membership, and structure were defined largely by its bylaws. The consortium structure was complex, consisting of multiple committees focused on strategies or issue areas (e.g., health education and promotion, clinical services, and neighborhood leadership development) and administrative areas (e.g., policy and oversight, sustainability, and evaluation). Many of the organizations that participated in the consortium contributed staff time and resources in-kind to the project. However, the number of members operating under more formal contracts with the project for the delivery of specific services typically ranged from 6 to 14 each year.

CDPH served not only as the leader of the consortium, but also as its grantee and fiscal agent. Because the consortium was not established as a separate legal entity, contracts created on behalf of the project were executed with the city. Similarly, funding obtained by the project was channeled through CDPH. Through the administrative committees, the consortium members had influence over what and how resources were divided among the members, but as with the contracts, the city had the ultimate authority for resource allocation, thus creating a more centralized system.

In contrast, human resource policies were more decentralized. Each member organization hired staff as appropriate to fulfill its project responsibilities. Guidelines were put in place for project staff to ensure consistency in such areas as job descriptions and salaries, but member organizations retained considerable latitude in their hiring and firing practices provided they complied with consortium bylaws, contracts, and other project policies where they pertained.

Whereas the HF/HS consortium operates much like other models of this type, its complexity can be linked in part to three distinct features. First, in many cases, alliances between public systems and private, nonprofit organizations require additional formality to ensure appropriate accountability and a more effective integration of the organizational cultures among these different organizational systems. Next, the federally mandated origin of the HF/HS consortium meant that the members had to establish an alliance based on their interpretations of what they thought the funder was requiring and to do so in a sufficiently comprehensive way to guarantee funding.

The comprehensive character of the project's approach to reducing infant mortality necessitated including efforts to address not only the medical aspects of the issue, but also other social and economic factors contributing to these negative outcomes. Whereas the overriding goal to integrate the resources of multiple organizations in an alliance to accomplish a goal that the organizations could not accomplish individually remains the same, under another set of circumstances, the consortium model can be operationalized much differently, as is demonstrated in the case of the Refugee Services Consortium in Houston, Texas.

Case Study: **Refugee Services Consortium**
Reporter: **YMCA of Greater Houston**

—OVERVIEW

The Refugee Services Consortium is an alliance of four agencies that offers programs and services to refugees resettling in the greater Houston area. The initial purpose of the alliance was to better organize refugee resettlement services and to use funding for these services more efficiently. The YMCA of Greater Houston was the alliance convener and served as its leader in the first year. After the first year, leadership of the alliance began rotating among the member agencies. The consortium's collaborative approach to refugee resettlement has resulted in staff sharing and joint housing operations. In addition, the consortium has enhanced relations between its member organizations, its primary funder, and other external stakeholders.

—PRECONDITIONS

Texas ranked fourth nationally in the number of refugees arriving in the state for the 15-year period beginning in October 1983 (Office of Refugee Resettlement, 1999). For much of this period, the funding for refugee resettlement programs had been stable, if not increasing. However, in the mid-1990s, funding began to decline, and the downward trend was expected to continue. The state was the primary funder of these services and, at the time, was dividing fewer available resources among the five organizations serving refugees in the greater Houston area.

In contrast to other areas in Texas, where one organization coordinated most of the refugee resettlement activities, Houston's refugee resettlement programs had a reputation for not working together. The agencies offered many complementary services, but these services were not organized. The contracting resource base was contributing to this situation by putting the agencies in competition with one another for funding.

As competition for resources began to increase, the agencies realized that if they did not partner, they would not all survive. In fact, if the resource pool available to fund refugee resettlement efforts declined much further, some of the agencies or some of their programs would be forced to close. The concept of an alliance was pursued as a way to demonstrate the agencies' capacity for collaboration as well as a way to organize funding and enhance service provision. The assumption of the member organizations was that forming an alliance would permit them to combine their resources, share staff, or otherwise integrate their programs to minimize the threat of agency closure. If, however, it became necessary for one or more agencies to reduce services, the alliance would allow these programs to close with minimal disruption to the refugees.

Historically, the YMCA was the strongest of the member agencies, but because of recent leadership changes, the organization had lost some of its influence with the state and other agencies. The YMCA's leaders saw convening an alliance composed of the various refugee resettlement agencies as one way to improve the agency's reputation at the state and local levels.

—PROCESS

The YMCA of Greater Houston was the leader in the effort to form the alliance. An agency supervisor in the area of refugee resettlement identified the need for interagency collaboration to increase information sharing and strengthen service linkages in the refugee resettlement domain. With the backing of the YMCA, she took the initiative to address it.

The first discussions among the refugee resettlement agencies began in 1994. The primary issue in these conversations was determining what each organization expected from participation in the alliance and how each organization could get its needs met in the process. Organizational members were particularly concerned about whether participation in the alliance would protect or hurt them. The process of negotiating this issue took several months. However, once it was resolved and members felt comfortable that the benefits of participation outweighed the risks, there was little need for negotiation around other membership issues, such as dividing roles and responsibilities. Similarly, there was only limited discussion about what type of alliance to form, and the alliance members chose the name Refugee Services Consortium because it just seemed to fit.

The consortium was established as an ongoing alliance, although members reassess the benefits of its continuation on a yearly basis. The consortium does not operate under bylaws. Formal letters of agreement stipulating leadership rotation, funding guidelines, and other governing policies and procedures are signed by the consortium members annually.

The YMCA was the leader of the consortium until the alliance was institutionalized. After the first year, leadership began to rotate annually.

The consortium's operating structure has evolved over time. When the consortium began, it had three primary committees. Two different staff groups met monthly to share information and collaborate on activities. These committees focused on separate aspects of refugee resettlement activities: resettlement and employment. After meeting this way for some time, the staff groups agreed to meet together on a monthly basis to respond more effectively and comprehensively to the interrelated issues of the refugees. The executives of the agencies met annually to focus on policy and as needed to address broader issues and conduct negotiations for the overall operation of the alliance. The executive committee established distribution percentages for the upcoming year's funding allocations and addressed consortiumwide policy issues.

Likewise, the way members communicate with each other has also changed. Initially, members shared information in consortium meetings only. As members got more comfortable with each other over time, they became more inclined to share information through less formal means. Members began exchanging information regularly by telephone and fax between the scheduled consortium meetings.

Initially, the alliance's purpose was to divide more efficiently the steady stream of funding available for refugee resettlement services among the agencies working in the area. The purpose has since broadened to include promoting a more seamless system of service delivery to refugees and their families and public advocacy.

The consortium does not employ a core staff to administer its activities. Staff from each member agency serve as organizational representatives to the consortium and carry out its tasks. However, the consortium hires and shares staff on a temporary basis as necessary to address the needs of individual refugee groups. Staff sharing is an important element of the consortium. Because the refugee populations entering Texas are continually and sometimes rapidly changing, the specific resources necessary to assist these culturally diverse groups vary from year to year. Individually, resettlement organizations have limited means to keep pace with these changes. For example, it may be impossible for one organization to maintain the appropriate number of Spanish-speaking caseworkers to assist 500-600 Cuban refugees on a temporary basis or to expect the same workers to facilitate the resettlement of Vietnamese refugees the next year. Staff sharing within the consortium is a more workable approach. Each organization transfers money to the consortium, and the agency or agencies with the largest expected caseloads hire the workers. After the workers are hired, the member agencies share their services. Each agency using the services contributes to the cost, which is determined proportionally according to its expected caseloads. The YMCA administers the billing and distribution of checks to member agencies because, as the first leader of the consortium, it initiated the process and has the infrastructure in place to continue these activities.

The primary strategy of the consortium is to present a united front to funders and other organizational stakeholders. Consequently, the agencies jointly apply for funding through the consortium. When funds are received, they are allocated to the member agencies according to prearranged percentages set forth in the annual letters of agreement. If an agency decides that it wants to apply for funds on its own (e.g., because the consortium has chosen not to pursue them or because they fit a specific organizational niche), it must bring the recommendation to the consortium for approval before proceeding.

Membership in the consortium is voluntary and at the discretion of the other members as determined through the annual membership renewal process. Letters of agreement are signed each year. At the renewal point, members may leave or may be asked to leave if they are not viewed by the others as contributing adequately to the alliance effort. Consortium membership has been relatively stable, in part because member agencies believe that withdrawing from the alliance might jeopardize their relationships with the state, which has strongly endorsed Houston's consortium approach to refugee resettlement. Only one consortium member has been asked to leave the alliance by the other members. The agency itself had become unstable and was unable to support the work of the alliance. Shortly after leaving the alliance, the agency stopped providing resettlement services.

Because there are no other agencies in the area that focus on the specific aspects of refugee resettlement that the consortium addresses, the consortium is not concerned about membership recruitment. However, even if there were, increasing membership would run counter to the purpose of the consortium, which is to maximize the use of available funding and other resources. Adding members would dilute consortium funding by requiring that the funds be divided among additional organizations.

Although the membership of the consortium is limited, the alliance has numerous environmental linkages that support its work. For instance, each local refugee resettlement agency operates as an affiliate of a national organization working in the domain of refugee resettlement. The national organizations provide funding support to their affiliated agencies and are primary sources of referrals. Therefore, securing the support of these organizations was an important aspect of the alliance development process.

—OUTCOMES

The Refugee Services Consortium incorporated external and internal assessments into its evaluation system. The consortium convinced the state to judge the success of its member organizations collectively, rather than continuing to assess the performance of each of its members individually. The agencies argued that this would reduce pressure on the individual agencies and create more incentive to collaborate.

Internally, the consortium monitors its performance monthly. A portion of the monthly consortium meetings is set aside for staff to compare agency statistics with overall performance standards. Each agency gauges its own and others' attainments relative to the consortium goal. At times, each of the member agencies has experienced periods in which its performance was substandard. However, as a collective effort, the consortium has remained successful. In the area of job placement, the key indicator of success from the state's perspective, the consortium is more effective as a whole than each organization was individually. This has yielded greater programmatic stability for the member organizations than they would have experienced on their own and validated the formation of the consortium.

Another positive outcome for consortium members is that they receive greater funding protection than they had prior to collaboration because each is guaranteed a percentage of the refugee resettlement funds obtained that year. One disadvantage of consortium membership is that because the percentage of the funding pool allocated to each agency is renegotiated annually, there are no guarantees on funding levels for individual agencies from year to year.

The support that the consortium received from the State of Texas has offered them greater political protection as well. Although it took a few years for the state to fully understand the benefits of the consortium strategy, the alliance's successes have led the state to push for even more collaboration among the agencies.

Refugees and their potential employers have also benefited from the agencies' collaboration. The refugee resettlement agencies had a reputation for fierce competition in securing jobs for the refugees who used their services. This created frustration for both the refugees and the organizations that made the jobs available. So, one of the strategies employed by the consortium was to combine the individual agencies' job lists. Now, each potential employer is assigned one agency as its contact for refugee job placement, but the consortium oversees all placement efforts. This improvement in the job placement process has benefited both the employer and the potential employee by making more and better jobs available.

More recent activity has led to similar benefits and eliminated some of the previous inefficiencies in the refugee housing process. Rather than each member agency continuing to operate individual shelters to provide temporary housing to refugees just entering the country, the consortium began operating joint housing units in several buildings throughout the city and purchasing food together to maximize resources.

In addition, the consortium has established a connection with agencies that provide complementary services for the refugee population. For instance, English as a Second Language (ESL) training and cultural orientation is a related area and separately funded aspect of the refugee resettlement work. A number of organizations apply for these funds. The consortium jointly selected a preferred provider from among them and actively supported the organization's bid for funding by signing a reciprocal referral agreement with the organization. The organization got funded, and the referral agreement has remained in place.

—*REPORTER'S REFLECTIONS AND LESSONS LEARNED*

From this process, the YMCA has learned several lessons that it has applied to its participation in other strategic alliances. First, building and maintaining strategic alliances is very hard and time-consuming work. The process does not necessarily come easily. Second, positive personal relationships among members are critical in determining a successful outcome. And, finally, ownership issues, even in nonprofit organizations, are real and tenacious. Protecting individual turf and seeing to it that agencies and individuals get recognition for contributions are issues that need to be addressed continually.

PRELIMINARY ANALYSIS:
SOME THOUGHTS ON DEVELOPMENT

Theoretical Perspectives

The needs of the member agencies for resource interdependence and strategic enhancement appear to be inextricably linked in the decision to form the consortium. The alliance was clearly seen by its members as a way to protect and share declining funding and to allow the member agencies more flexibility to restructure themselves organizationally so that the services they offered to refugees would continue. The agencies all viewed the services they offered to refugees as critical in assisting the refugees and their families with their transition to living in the United States. To preserve these services, the need to maintain consistent access to resources (resource interdependence) was as important as the need to protect the existence of agency resettlement services and maintain a seamless system of service delivery for their consumers (strategic enhancement).

The development of the consortium can also be viewed easily from the perspectives of environmental validity and operational efficiency. Enhancing agency credibility with the state was an important factor in stabilizing refugee resettlement funding and service delivery, especially in the view of the YMCA. Forming a consortium of the area refugee resettlement agencies would help the members counteract their reputation for lack of organization in the delivery of services, a perception held by both the state and local agencies. Indeed, the consortium would become an essential element in securing further funding and in maintaining relationships with potential employers and other organizations in the community that were needed to support the resettlement process. It also led to positive changes for the consortium members in the way their performance was measured by their funders. All of these outcomes focused on increasing legitimacy with organizational stakeholders to support the development of the alliance from the perspective of environmental validity.

The desire of the member agencies for operational efficiency became more evident as funding stabilized. Once the immediate survival of their services was no longer threatened, the members began to focus their attention on how to maximize the utilization of their resources. As they became more comfortable with each other and saw each other less as competitors in the service delivery arena and more as partners, the agencies began to integrate their services more comprehensively. They implemented protocols for staff sharing and engaged in collaborative housing ventures and food-purchasing initiatives, taking greater advantage of the opportunities for economies of scale made possible through the alliance.

Alliance Model

Little consideration was given in this case to the creation of a specific alliance model. In fact, the consortium simply evolved. This gradual evolution in defining a structure is not uncommon for an alliance. However, the process goes beyond the basic principle of "form follows function" (Chandler, 1962).

As discussed in Chapter 3, function, an aspect of the alliance's purpose, is only one element affecting the decisions made about the alliance's structure. The other six alliance components—leadership, membership, linkages, strategy, systems, and tasks—also affect this decision. For example, the extent to which each member organization is willing to relinquish its autonomy—an aspect of membership—is another important determinant of the alliance model chosen. The Refugee Services Consortium members saw relinquishing a moderately high degree of autonomy as necessary for survival. If members had been unwilling to integrate their resources and other systems to this extent, a less formal alliance model would have been chosen.

The consortium was not created as a separately incorporated organization, although it does operate as a distinct entity, with one or more agencies acting on its behalf, for the purposes of receiving and disbursing money, negotiating referral agreements, operating a joint housing facility, evaluating program outcomes, and engaging in other activities. The operational definition of the alliance as one entity is an important characteristic of the consortium and other collaborative models that increases the interdependence among the members and differentiates these models from cooperative or coordinated alliances.

Although the consortium is governed largely by annual letters of agreement signed by its members, these agreements promote significant interdependence among the agencies and pose potentially serious risks to the members as well. As structured, the executives of each member agency comprise the executive committee, and each has an equal vote. This committee is responsible for determining what percentage of the state refugee resettlement allocation for the upcoming year will go to each agency and has the authority to say whether or not a member agency can apply for refugee resettlement funding outside the consortium. Thus, the level of funding for each agency is, in effect, decided by all of the consortium members, demonstrating a moderately high degree of organizational integration.

Continued membership in the alliance can also be seen as being at the discretion of the other members. In an environment where the primary funding for refugee resettlement services came from one source and the funder strongly supported the consortium concept, being asked to leave the consortium has potentially serious service delivery implications. Likewise, the consortium members are responsible to the funder for a single set of outcome measures. Within the consortium, each agency has its own target goals, but the success of each of the refugee resettlement programs is dependent upon how all of the agencies perform collectively, again increasing the interdependence among the agencies.

Phases of Development

The role that the YMCA played in the development of the alliance is consistent with the evolution of a consortium model. The YMCA was the convening organization and served as the alliance leader in the assembling and ordering phases. It identified a need and took the initiative to bring appropriate parties together to decide how to address it. The YMCA continues to manage the alliance's financial matters, such as receiving and disbursing money, but as the convener, it does so on behalf of the consortium. Individual organizational leadership of the executive committee rotates annually, but each organization maintains one vote in the committee. Thus, the formal leadership of the alliance is shared.

The assembling phase of the alliance took several months. The members shared similar concerns about funding and the lack of integration of programs and services. However, the major thrust of the phase was on clarifying members' expectations about what they wanted from the alliance and on reaching some consensus on how the agencies could meet these needs by working together. Against the backdrop of an already unstable funding environment and a historically competitive relationship among the agencies offering refugee resettlement services, it took time to establish enough trust in the group so that members felt comfortable agreeing to move forward with the alliance. The issue at the core of these discussions was ensuring that participation in the alliance would benefit the members rather than harm them. Throughout the discussion, the agencies were continually reassessing the benefit-cost ratio associated with involvement in the alliance.

Once these issues were resolved at a satisfactory level for prospective members, the alliance moved into the ordering phase. The members had invested a lot of energy and time in establishing a shared understanding of what the alliance could do to benefit the members and developing a foundation of trust on which to build the alliance. Therefore, they did not feel it was critical to spend much time negotiating the details of the alliance that are typically part of the ordering phase.

The initial ordering phase of the consortium focused largely on issues such as deciding that leadership would rotate and that letters of agreement would be renegotiated annually. The members also had to determine how they would present the consortium to the state and to its other stakeholders. Yet because of the decisions made in this phase, each year, the consortium must revisit the ordering phase of development, at least briefly, to establish standards for the coming year. This means electing a new leader, agreeing on membership, formulating resource allocation percentages, and so on. In addition, each time the consortium shares staff or engages in a new activity such as joint purchasing, it must return to the ordering phase to establish the appropriate responsibilities, how resources will be allocated, and other parameters.

This arrangement has worked, in part, because the consortium has gradually increased its structural integration. The alliance focused first on collectively dealing with the pressing need to stabilize funding. As the benefits of the partnership have become more evident—and, correspondingly, as trust continued to grow—the members began adding new joint activities to the consortium effort. Most recently, they integrated their temporary housing and food purchasing programs to increase the efficiency with which they administer and deliver these services to the refugees and their families. The gradual addition of activities that increased organizational interdependence allowed the members to build and negotiate the partnership one step at a time.

The consortium was structured so that most of the activities indicative of the performing phase are carried out by agency staff working in the refugee resettlement programs. The performing phase began with two separate staff committees: one focused on resettlement programs and one focused on employment. However, this approach was eventually identified as inefficient. Resettlement and employment issues were interconnected for the refugees and their families, so arbitrarily separating them in the consortium did not support the goal of creating a more seamless system of service delivery. The committees were therefore combined, and the staff began jointly addressing programmatic issues and evaluating program outcomes. The staffs of the member agencies meet monthly, but communication among them occurs regularly between meetings.

One key activity for the consortium in the performing phase has been the establishment of environmental linkages to support its work. The alliance has engaged in a referral agreement with a provider of English as a Second Language services and has created a uniform plan for how prospective employers will interface with the consortium members in hiring their consumers. These organizations are not members of the alliance, but the relationships that the consortium has established with them further promote the alliance's goal of improving the system of service delivery for refugees and their families.

Another important aspect of the performing phase for the Refugee Services Consortium—and, ideally, for alliance efforts in general—is the regular focus on monitoring program outcomes. Reviewing the progress of the member agencies in relation to individual and consortium goals on a monthly basis gives the members ongoing opportunities to make midcourse corrections, if necessary, to ensure that the alliance is performing effectively in terms of the services it is delivering to its consumers.

Unfortunately, as is the case with the evaluation of most alliance-based projects, the consortium's formal evaluation systems focus solely on outcomes. They do not include formal assessments of the effectiveness of the alliance process. The executive committee informally evaluates the process each year when it develops new letters of agreement, at which time members may be asked to leave. However, as will be discussed in Chapter 11, most alliances, regardless of their position on the alliance continuum, would benefit from a more strategic process evaluation.

The assessment of the consortium, in conjunction with the negotiation of letters of agreement, demonstrates the iterative nature of the consortium's development. This process, albeit brief, moves the consortium through an annual transition from performing to transforming, and as letters of agreement are renewed, through assembling and ordering again. This process requires members to recommit to the alliance and provides them with formal opportunities to alter the various components of the consortium to strengthen or otherwise modify it. This process of cycling back through previously completed phases may not be as obvious in many other alliance efforts, but the concept is the same. When the alliance faces a change in any one of its components, it must undertake a corresponding evaluation of the other components to ensure that they remain aligned in such a way that the alliance continues to function most productively for its members and its other stakeholders.

Chapter 8

NETWORKS

As stated at the outset of this book, the changing nature of service reform in the health and human service fields has had a dramatic impact on why and how HSOs decide to work together. No place is this more evident in recent years than in the case of networks. Over the past two decades, several significant trends have emerged in the environment in which social service and mental health providers were operating and have led many organizations to pursue strategic alliances that they might not have considered earlier. The impact of managed care was primary among these.

The 1980s saw the rising movement in the health arena to a targeted focus on lowering the rate at which health care costs were rising. Health care payment and delivery were restructured to reflect the implementation of strategies that lowered cost, largely through adjustments to service use and the elimination of services perceived to be unnecessary. This restructuring, while incorporating a wide variety of strategies, is generally known as managed care.

As managed care became a dominant force in shaping physical and behavioral health care and, most recently, child welfare service delivery, strategic alliances were created to respond. These alliances were often called networks. However, unlike the less formal alliances that previously had been called networks, the complexities of integrating provider services to respond to the mandates of payors moved these managed care networks from the first quarter of the strategic alliance continuum to the third. Thus, in line with managed care, networks have evolved from loosely connected cooperative systems of organizations largely sharing information to more formal structures that resemble consortia and joint ventures.

There are generally two types of networks, and they vary depending on the kinds of organizations participating in them. *Horizontal* networks involve organizations that provide similar services, and *vertical* networks involve organizations offering different services. Horizontal networks may concentrate on child welfare services, whereas vertical networks combine a wide range of service options such as hospital- and clinic-based mental health services and child welfare into one system of care (Emenhiser et al., 1998). Yet regardless of type, networks are integrated service systems that seek to improve service delivery by deepening or broadening the scope of services available to their consumers. Ultimately, such networks are formed "to enhance efficiencies . . . and/or negotiate managed care contracts directly with payors" (Murphy, 1995, p. G-5).

Specific network structures vary but are frequently established as new legal entities that exist to administer the collaborative service delivery systems. Where the network is separately incorporated, a central office generally manages these activities, and member organizations share ownership of the network through representation on its board of trustees. Because the legal requirements for creating such structures differ from state to state, it is crucial that organizations considering participation in integrated service delivery networks consult legal advice before proceeding and throughout the development process.

Articles of incorporation, bylaws, formal contracts, and other legally binding agreements define the leadership, membership, and systems of integration such as resource procurement and allocation. Member organizations usually retain their own identities, governing boards, and independence around their core functions not directly related to the network. However, such organizational independence may actually be a function of financial or legal necessities rather than a matter of practice preference (McLaughlin, 1998).

Another related structure, sometimes called a network, is a *management service organization*. The management service organization is created to generate greater organizational efficiency by integrating the management or administrative functions of multiple HSOs into one entity (Arsenault, 1998). Management service organizations operate like federations or associations, combining management information systems, quality assurance, financial services, contracting, or other administrative functions. Yet they do so in a more comprehensive way and through formal contractual relationships that bear greater resemblance to integrated service delivery networks, but with a concentrated focus on administrative consolidation.

Catholic Social Service of Northern and Central Arizona (CSS) participates as a member of the Full Circle Healthcare Network, a countywide behavioral health network. The network began in 1997 when the executives of CSS and the executives of several other organizations with compatible values met to discuss the changes taking place in the behavioral health arena in the state of Arizona. They decided to pursue the formation of a network to enhance their service delivery capacity with the goal of securing additional funding to provide these services throughout the county.

Full Circle was incorporated in the state of Arizona as a separate organization. The network has applied for tax-exempt status and is awaiting approval on its application.

The network has 13 organizational members and is classified as a vertical network. In addition to CSS, members include hospitals, residential service facilities, behavioral health emergency service and outpatient service providers, and addiction services programs. Together, they provide a range of child and adolescent mental health and psychiatry services, drug and alcohol treatment, child welfare services, and services for seriously mentally ill clients.

Regardless of size, each organization has one member, and thus, one vote on the network's governing board. The members elect a board chair and other network officers from the membership for 1-year terms. Considerable attention was given to shared organizational values in forming the network, so governance and decision making have not been significant issues for the alliance, although with 13 members, it occasionally takes a lot of time before they reach consensus.

To create the infrastructure necessary to begin operating, the members had to capitalize the network. To do this, each member organization contributed between $11,000 and $25,000 to the network. The amount of money each member contributed was based on the percentage of business each organization had in the behavioral health arena. These funds were used to hire the network director and a consultant to assist in network-related activities and to subsidize the cost of developing other systems. For example, the network has created a series of clinical protocols to guide service delivery and has established central management information and intake systems.

Because the network is a legally incorporated entity, its staff are employed by the network, not through one of the member organizations on behalf of the network. In addition, its contracts, such as leases for office space and equipment, are executed with the network directly. Full Circle is an example of a vertical network. However, horizontal networks are also common in the behavioral health domain. The case of FamilyHelp illustrates how one such network developed in response to the particular needs of its members.

Case Study:	**FamilyHelp, a behavioral health network**
Reporter:	**Central City Multi-Service Agency**[1]

OVERVIEW

The family behavioral health network was created as a collaborative alliance among six social service and mental health agencies to integrate similar services across a large metropolitan area. It was formed in response to changes in the reimbursement of the behavioral health services that those agencies had traditionally provided for low-income families. The partners created a new organization, FamilyHelp, to implement the core operations of the alliance, and each organization is a member/owner of the network. FamilyHelp competes for contracts with both local, public behavioral health payors and private, commercial insurers. FamilyHelp members provide contracted services. Excess revenue generated by contracts is split between FamilyHelp (for reinvestment) and its six member/owners. FamilyHelp governance is provided by the executive directors of the six member/owner organizations.

PRECONDITIONS

Managed care strategies began to be implemented in the mental health field in the early 1990s. The six agencies that created FamilyHelp experienced the advent of managed care in comparable ways. Each received direct reimbursement for their behavioral health services from two sources, commercial insurance companies and public funding authorities. Both commercial insurance companies and public funding authorities implemented managed care strategies, but commercial insurers' managed care practices affected the FamilyHelp agencies more directly.

First, the commercial insurers lowered the rate at which they were willing to reimburse behavioral health services. Second, they reduced the number of providers with which they were willing to contract. Social service and mental health agencies consequently experienced a reduction in both the number of individuals referred to them for service and the reimbursement rates provided for those few services that were provided. For the six ·agencies that created FamilyHelp, these reductions equated to roughly 20% of their behavioral health revenue over a 5-year period from 1990 to 1995.

Second, public funders of mental health services became increasingly aware of the popularity of managed care strategies as an approach to containing costs and ensuring the best use of limited resources. Elected officials were aware of the perceived success of managed care in the private sector and urged local funding authorities to consider strategies like managed care in the public sector. As such, in 1994, the local mental health funder announced the results of a strategic plan in which the cornerstone would be to maximize the effective use of public revenue by reducing the number of agencies with which it contracted. The plan also identified that successful contractors would be those with service and geographic breadth.

In effect, local agencies that did not have those characteristics were threatened with losing their contracts. On average, the six agencies in FamilyHelp derived 40% of their annual operating income from contracts with the local mental health funding authority, and they could not lose this revenue and still survive.

Several other preconditions also informed the agencies' decision to pursue a strategic alliance. For the agencies combined, gross United Way revenue had decreased approximately 25% over the previous 5 years. Furthermore, five new specialty mental health agencies, including one for profit, had been established recently in the community. Each of the member agencies perceived some form of competition from these new specialty agencies.

The six agencies that created FamilyHelp first came together as a result of the close personal and professional relationships the agency executives shared with each other. Most of them had been in their positions for at least 10 years, and all had started and built their careers in the same community. They came together, informally at first, to discuss their shared concerns about the challenges each organization was experiencing because of these changes in the external environment.

—PROCESS

In these discussions, the organizations identified common challenges each faced in achieving its mission and goals. In particular, they were concerned about projected downward revenue trends that raised troubling questions about each agency's long-term future. Analysis of this theme revealed some deeper issues for the partners that required a concerted response for the agencies to be competitive in the managed care environment.

Commercial insurance revenue had declined because none of the agencies was positioned to meet the provider needs of those insurers. That is, each lacked the capacity to provide adequate service volume to accept lower reimbursement rates. In addition, each had insufficient capacity to meet the broad needs of commercial insurers. The change in direction from the public mental health funder was problematic because each agency on its own lacked the geographic reach that the funder needed from providers, and again, each separately lacked capacity. Finally, the agencies had not identified any successful strategies to replace the lost revenue from declining United Way funding.

It quickly became apparent to the executives that a strategic alliance was the best possible option. The agencies offered similar behavioral health services, such as outpatient counseling, short-term employee assistance programs, and outpatient substance abuse counseling, although some did so on a relatively small scale. The executives agreed that the primary issues identified through their analysis could be addressed if each of the six increased its service and geographic breadth. The development of sufficient additional service capacity and geographic distribution individually was impractical; the services that were needed were already available among these other organizations. Through an alliance, the executives decided that the six organizations could create the capacity they needed to meet the needs of the public funder and compete for commercial managed care contracts.

Once the executives agreed to the strategic alliance in concept, they determined that putting one together would require them to meet more regularly and more formally. The directors informed their boards that alliance planning was under way and solicited feedback from the trustees to determine whether they considered the plan appropriate and what concerns or parameters they would bring to the establishment of a strategic alliance.

Having identified common issues in their initial discussions, the executives began considering what type of alliance would best meet their needs. To do this, the directors articulated the goals of the alliance, which reflected an interest in expanded geographic coverage and service capacity. In addition, they identified a priority of generating revenue to support each agency's behavioral health activities. The discussion also yielded a clear understanding that each agency wanted to retain its identity and autonomy. Finally, although the executives agreed that behavioral health would be the primary focus of the alliance, they acknowledged that this was only one dimension of each agency's service focus.

The executives agreed that the type of alliance best suited to the individual and collective goals of the six agencies was a network. The executives decided to establish the network as a new organization, and they retained legal counsel to assess the range of structural options available to them and the corresponding impact of possible decisions. Because the members had started as equal partners in the process—despite differences in the size of each organization—the executives determined that their collaboration would be best supported if that equality was maintained. Consequently, they chose an arrangement in which the six members would each pay an equal fee to become a full voting member in the new organization.

The members agreed that the new organization, which they named FamilyHelp, would be the agent that would represent the wide array of behavioral health services that the six organizations provided. FamilyHelp would advocate with commercial insurers and public funders to generate contracts and service referrals based on location and type of services provided by all six organizations. In this way, the members would be able to address the primary threats to continued service provision raised by commercial insurers and public funders. Through this formal alliance, they could offer the service and geographic scope requested by public funders and the lower unit cost per service required of commercial insurers.

The executives determined that FamilyHelp would function as a gatekeeper through which service referrals would be made to the member organizations. Referrals were made based on a match between client needs and both agency expertise and geographic location. The six directors created a committee of the senior clinical staff from each of their organizations to address the wide range of service delivery integration questions that needed to be resolved in order to provide seamless, consistent, quality service. For the next few months, the committee wrote service protocols and considered other details necessary to determine the overall shape of service delivery. They presented their recommendations to the executives for review as they progressed.

One of the final issues that the members had to negotiate prior to establishing the network was how revenue generated by the organization would be received and distributed among the six partners. This issue was among the most difficult to decide. In the most practical terms, revenue was an underlying theme in the service conversations that had been taking place among the partner organizations. All needed service revenue in order to operate. To determine how to distribute revenue, the six partners again sought legal counsel and revisited the goals of the alliance.

It was clear that the revenue needed to be distributed for three core activities: the direct service provided by partner organizations, the administrative requirements of the direct service provided by each of the partners, and the administrative services provided by FamilyHelp. The executives agreed that they would develop a rate of reimbursement for all types of services provided through FamilyHelp contracts, not unlike rates already paid to partner organizations by commercial insurers.

Furthermore, they agreed that FamilyHelp would receive a percentage of each contract that was successfully negotiated. That rate would be used to pay the cost of operating FamilyHelp and allow for reinvestment in additional capacity, if needed.

Whatever revenue remained would be distributed to each of the partner organizations based on the amount of service that partner had provided under a particular contract in a given contract year. That arrangement guaranteed that direct service was adequately paid for and provided additional resources based both on profitability and service participation. Moreover, the partners agreed that the arrangement was consistent with the goals of creating FamilyHelp.

After resolving these issues, the executives, with the help of their legal counsel, created bylaws to document their decisions and clarify how the alliance would be structured. The bylaws specified membership requirements, governance, resource procurement and distribution methods, decision making, and other features that would direct the operation of the new organization. At this time, and again with the assistance of their legal counsel, the members filed the necessary papers with the state to incorporate the network and, considering the potential for expanding the role of the network in the future, decided not to pursue tax-exempt status for the alliance.

Once the network was incorporated as an independent organization and the members had a plan for how it would function, the executives began creating the administrative infrastructure to support the alliance. The executives hired a director for the organization. The director served as the primary contact with public funders and commercial insurers for contracts and service and supervised the staff and the development of other systems as necessary. These included a common management information system through which to link client records at the network level. The organization hired an accountant to monitor revenue and expenses and coordinate billings, and it hired intake staff to receive phone-based client referrals and direct them as appropriate to one of the six member organizations. Once the staff was in place, FamilyHelp began operating.

—OUTCOMES

FamilyHelp was created 3 years ago, and to date, its outcomes have been mixed. The network approach has worked effectively as a strategy to increase commercial insurance referrals. The six organizations clearly addressed what those insurers were looking for in behavioral health service. Service volume has increased. However, service reimbursement rates remain low. FamilyHelp has seen limited excess revenue to distribute among its partners for increases in service volume that have been generated. Yet FamilyHelp partners are providing much greater commercial service volume than their peers in the nonprofit sector who have not entered into alliances and remain moderate to small providers.

FamilyHelp has positioned its members effectively with public funders. The FamilyHelp partners are seen as innovative and responsive to changing funder and community needs. The public funders have moved slowly in the implementation of new approaches to contracting owing, in part, to greater ambivalence in the public sector than in the private sector about moving from contracting with many local providers to fewer, larger providers.

Perhaps the area of greatest challenge for the FamilyHelp members has been coming to consensus about clinical service delivery. Senior staff in each organization have been trained differently and approach clinical service delivery differently. These differences of opinion and practice have led to uneven implementation of service protocols at the six member agencies. On several occasions, payors objected to service delivered in ways that differed from the protocols they had previously been provided. Ongoing disagreements on this issue created threats to FamilyHealth's ability to maintain contracts with commercial insurers. However, the executives of the member organizations continue to negotiate this issue.

FamilyHelp is also working to put a more formal evaluation system in place. With its new management information system operating well, it hopes to do a more comprehensive job at monitoring how the creation of the alliance has benefited the consumers whom the organizations serve. In addition, it has added a regular agenda item to its board meetings: ongoing conversations about how the process of working together is benefiting and challenging its members.

—REPORTER'S REFLECTIONS AND LESSONS LEARNED

Through this experience, the members of FamilyHelp learned several lessons about developing integrated service delivery networks. First, member organizations need to recognize at the outset that the network development process will be time-consuming. As such, they need to acknowledge that their leaders have other important activities that compete for their time, but they must agree to prioritize attendance at regular meetings to give full attention to collectively negotiating the details of the development process. Moreover, the members need to cede to the common goals of the network throughout the process, or they will be continually challenged in achieving them.

Finally, because members continue to retain control of their individual organizations outside the scope of the alliance, it is crucial that the network carefully develop a consistent plan to govern its operations. Administrative staff may be hired by the alliance, but direct service staff usually are not. Thus, different staff are accountable to different organizational standards and protocols and are not subject to consistent authority. Therefore, if the policies under which staff will implement services, for example, are not clearly defined and agreed to at the network level, serious challenges can result and may threaten the sustainability of the alliance.

PRELIMINARY ANALYSIS: SOME THOUGHTS ON DEVELOPMENT

Theoretical Perspectives

In this case, six organizations came together to address challenges that each was experiencing due to changes in the external environment. Many of the changes were the result of the growing impact of managed care on delivery and third-party payment of behavioral health services. These changes threatened each organization's capacity to continue to provide the services that it was the mission of each to provide, and as the alliance progressed, it became evident that the reasons each had for pursuing the alliance were nearly identical.

From the resource interdependence perspective, the organizations shared a need to maintain the resources that paid for the services they delivered. This was especially true in view of the fact that the substantive contracting and funding changes corresponding with managed behavioral health care were occurring just as the organizations were experiencing a significant downward trend in their United Way allocations.

Viewing the formation of the alliance from the environmental validity perspective, the agencies were responding to the changing requirements of the funding institutions that provided the majority of their behavioral health funds. The move to a managed care approach for funding behavioral health services led these funders to specify different parameters on which to base their resource allocation decisions. To maintain their legitimacy with the funders, and thus qualify for continued contracts, the agencies needed to respond to the new service delivery priorities set forth by the commercial insurers and the public funders.

The partners realized that one of the key features required of the organizations that sought to be competitive under the managed care system was service breadth, in terms of both type and geographic scope. This consideration is central to the strategic enhancement perspective of alliance formation and, combined with additional competition from new specialty mental health agencies, was a significant motivator in the formation of FamilyHelp. At the core of this perspective, the organizations were seeking to enhance and expand their services to increase their chances of survival in a changing and more competitive marketplace.

Alliance Model

Collectively, the member agencies undertook a planning process in which they analyzed their mutual challenges. That planning process correctly identified the environmental sources of their difficulties. Their recommendation to create FamilyHelp was the strategy they pursued to address the environmental threats to each organization's future.

The choice of the network model for the FamilyHelp alliance was consistent with the members' alliance goals. With a network, the six agencies could create a new organization in which each of them was an equal partner. The new organization would exist to accomplish the business goals of the alliance: to organize and represent the capacity of all six members in the behavioral health service area, while still maintaining a significant level of organizational autonomy beyond the scope of the alliance. FamilyHelp could legally be classified as a joint venture, an alliance model that will be discussed in more detail in the next chapter, but its focus on creating a continuum of care in response to the impact of managed care on behavioral health care corresponds with the niche that is uniquely referred to as an integrated service network.

The desire for members to expand service breadth and also retain their autonomy were accomplished, in part, by specifically focusing the joint effort on behavioral health services. However, these goals reduced the potential alliance models available to the members. More informal alliances, such as affiliations, federations, and coalitions, were structured too loosely to provide the integrated service provision capacity necessary to meet the demands of commercial and public payors. In contrast, the most formal alliance types, such as mergers, were too restrictive, eliminating identity and autonomy for at least some of the partners by consolidating the full range of services each partner provided into one organization while dissolving the others. The members did not perceive these steps to be necessary to accomplish their goals. That is, if each wanted to affect only one aspect of the work they did—in this case, behavioral health—it was unnecessary to bring all other services together into one, merged organizational entity.

Phases of Development

The assembling phase began with a series of informal meetings among the executives. This investigation generated the recognition that their organizations shared common issues and concerns in each one's attempt to achieve its mission and goals. In response, they collectively examined the more specific reasons why each was having difficulty adapting to the environmental changes and identified strategies to enable them to accomplish their missions and goals more successfully.

For each of the organizations, annual revenue from commercial insurance and the United Way had declined steadily in previous years. In addition, all were concerned that long-term public support for mental health programs was threatened because the funder's direction was inconsistent with theirs, and they felt that their agencies did not have the capacity to respond individually. However, together, they determined that by allying the six organizations, they would be better positioned to meet service and distribution needs.

Two significant elements that characterized the network's assembling phase and contributed to its success were the positive relationships that existed among the six executives and the similarity of the agencies' reasons for pursuing the alliance. The strong relationships among the members provided a foundation of mutual trust and respect that often takes considerable time to develop in the alliance formation process. Moreover, because the agencies were relinquishing some of their autonomy in the creation of the alliance, these established personal relationships combined with the congruence of their organizational goals to minimize the negotiation that is frequently necessary in getting potential alliance members to understand each other and build the relationship.

Once the decision was made to proceed with the formation of the alliance, the executives who served as its leaders sought input and approval from their boards of trustees before continuing. Although boards need to be aware of any strategic alliance activities, the more formal and integrated the chosen model is, the greater the potential risks to the organizations, and therefore, the more important it is to involve the board early in the process.

The next step in the alliance's development, and the one that corresponded with its move from assembling to ordering, was for the executives to begin considering the structure that the alliance would take. In this case, the executives defined their goals and priorities for the venture more specifically, which included each organization retaining its autonomy and identity, and reviewed these in the context of the various strategic alliance alternatives. Reaching consensus that the best alternative was a network, they decided to structure it by creating a new organization that would equitably represent the capacity and interest of the six partners. Beyond that, they had to determine how this new organization would be governed and what its relationship would be to the six members. Because of the complexities of these decisions and their significant potential to affect the operations of the member organizations, the executives appropriately sought legal advice to assist throughout the ordering phase.

The six executives spent much of the subsequent time determining how best to administer the new organization and how to organize integrated service provision so that consumers experienced service delivery as seamless. At this point, the executives broadened the input in the network ordering process by involving senior clinical staff from each of the organizations. The staff committee reported to the executive group and developed the protocols that would direct service delivery across the network. The participation of the staff at this time ensured that the integration of services was organized from the perspective of those who dealt with consumer issues on a routine basis. Dictating the specifics of service integration from the highest administrative levels would have likely resulted in a service delivery plan that was not grounded in the real-life experiences of the agencies' consumers.

The members created FamilyHelp to function as the liaison between public funders, commercial insurers, and the six member agencies. In addition, it served as an intermediary for clients initially referred to FamilyHelp for service. Consequently, the establishment of the alliance required investment in administrative infrastructure to support its operation and goals. Therefore, once the alliance was incorporated, it transitioned into the performing phase. At this point, the executives—now the network's governing board—hired staff and began developing other systems to carry out the network's tasks.

The FamilyHelp network has shown moderate success. The organizations have increased behavioral health revenue from commercial insurance companies and have been recognized as innovative by their primary public funders. In that way, the creation of the network was an effective strategy for addressing the concerns raised by each organization. At the same time, FamilyHealth struggled with issues endemic to alliance models that require collaboration but do not fully centralize control. Senior clinical staff from each of the partner organizations worked together to develop and implement joint service delivery protocols, but persistent disagreements about clinical practice interfered with FamilyHelp's capacity to create the consistent and predictable integrated service delivery system that is critical to its credibility with both commercial insurers and public funders. In this area, the absence of a central decision maker created challenges to the successful implementation of the network.

The current focus of the alliance on improving conversations about the alliance process at the governance level is one step in addressing this issue. However, it is equally important that the senior clinical staff and the direct line staff from each of the member organizations also have regular opportunities to identify and work through the issues they are facing in implementing the work of the alliance. The goal of this dialogue at all levels needs to be supporting continued conversations about how participating in the alliance is benefiting and challenging its members. In this way, the network will create more opportunities to strengthen the alliance, not only to support the member organizations, but also to provide even better services to the community.

NOTE

1. Identifying information was removed from this case at the request of the reporter.

Chapter 9

JOINT VENTURES

The term *joint venture* is often used in a general way to describe a broad range of collaborative relationships and can include the consortia and network models discussed in Chapters 7 and 8. For example, the joint venture has been defined as "a specific project or program developed and operated by two or more parties for their mutual benefit" (Emenhiser et al., 1998, p. 41).

The broad use of this term is due, in part, to the fact that there are a number of ways to legally structure a joint venture. Sometimes, they are created through mutual contracts, resembling consortia or networks. Frequently, they are established through the creation of a legally sanctioned partnership or the formation of a new corporation. The establishment of legal partnerships and new corporations creates more formal and integrated collaborative relationships, although as noted earlier, more formal networks may look very much like this type of joint venture. Acknowledging that consortia and networks could be considered forms of joint ventures, the emphasis of the joint venture model described in this chapter is on the more formal structural arrangements that are not generally characteristic of these other alliance models.

In a joint venture, two or more organizations form a new, legally defined entity. The member organizations maintain joint ownership of the alliance as the mechanism for carrying out specific tasks or developing and providing certain services, thus focusing the alliance's purpose in a single system of operations and, in many cases, insulating the individual operations of the member organizations from the alliance's liabilities.

The joint venture model differs from the network model largely in the purpose of the project. A network focuses on creating the infrastructure through which to offer a continuum of services on an ongoing basis. In a joint venture, the project can be time-limited and is often more narrowly defined. In addition, joint ventures tend to be more tightly and formally organized than do the other collaborative models.

Equal ownership of the joint venture is often exercised in the form of a joint governance board on which member organizations serve with equal representation. Thus, members share the assets and liabilities of the alliance. At the same time, the member organizations of a joint venture retain their individual identities and their own governance bodies, which maintain authority over organizational matters that extend beyond the scope of the alliance.

Like other collaborative models, joint ventures are formal arrangements directed at achieving a common goal through the sharing of a full range of member resources, including funding and staff. A joint venture, however, can be one of the most complex of the collaborative structures, often bordering on coadunation in the degree to which member organizations are integrated. For these reasons, joint ventures often involve participation of only a limited number of members.

Specific legal entities that are used to structure joint ventures include a general or limited partnership, a Limited Liability Company, or a separately incorporated organization. Each of these structural arrangements offers members different legal protections against liabilities and tax ramifications (Arsenault, 1998; Murphy, 1995). Given the serious legal and operational implications for each of these alternatives, organizations considering participation in a joint venture are strongly encouraged to seek expert legal counsel prior to formation.

Membership in a joint venture is defined by bylaws, contracts, operating agreements, and other legally binding documents, thus reducing member flexibility in executing certain tasks. Because joint ventures do not require the complete integration of one organization into another, as in the coadunation process, members can extricate themselves relatively easily from a joint venture. However, when these alliances are tied to the completion of a specific project, they may be established to dissolve if one of the member organizations withdraws. These and other guidelines should be defined clearly in the joint venture's governing documents.

An example of a joint venture is the HealthRays Alliance, in which the Benjamin Rose Institute in Cleveland, Ohio, was a founding member. The purpose of the alliance was to develop a strategy for maintaining the independence and financial viability of nonprofit long-term health providers that perceived the threat of losing their constituencies as a result of managed care and health care reform. The ability of such organizations to survive would help address the emerging community issues of reduced choice and, sometimes, reduced availability of care for consumers by providing acceptable alternative long-term care opportunities.

HealthRays Alliance has 25 member organizations and represents the largest nonprofit long-term health providers in the region. The member organizations all have compatible missions, and individually, they provide housing, home-based health care, and/or long-term care for elderly residents in five counties in northeast Ohio.

The joint venture was established as a separately incorporated taxable organization owned entirely by its nonprofit members. The governing board of the alliance is composed of the top institutional executive from each of the member organizations. The alliance was initially created for a minimum of three years and continues to operate with dues paid by the member organizations. Any member can withdraw from the alliance upon 180-day notice. In doing so, the organization forfeits all benefits associated with membership in the alliance, but the alliance does not dissolve if a member leaves.

Some of the benefits of participation include strategies focused on assisting member organizations as a group to improve service quality, reduce service costs, and increase revenues. The alliance members take part in regular financial and medical forums focused on issues directly related to the provision of long-term care, and they use common software to monitor service provision and resident satisfaction. Much like a network, the alliance negotiates contracts with Medicare HMOs on behalf of its member organizations. The alliance employs four staff to oversee these activities.

The alliance has developed other, related joint ventures in which members can choose to participate. One of these joint ventures is the Health-Rays Pharmacy, LLC. The pharmacy is a Limited Liability Company that was developed as a partnership between the HealthRays Group (i.e., the HealthRays Alliance and a subset of its member organizations) and Omnicare, Inc., a large, national, publicly held pharmacy services corporation. The HealthRays Alliance and its members own 50% of the joint venture, and Omnicare, Inc. owns the remaining 50%.

By definition, Limited Liability Companies are for-profit corporations. However, they offer benefits in some circumstances for nonprofit organizations. By establishing the pharmacy as a Limited Liability

Company, the member/owners gained protection from liabilities without having to create a newly incorporated organization. In the case of HealthRays, the pharmacy provides one way for alliance members to reduce prescription costs and generate profits to support the HealthRays alliance without jeopardizing their nonprofit status.

Limited Liability Companies provide one way to create a joint venture. However, as discussed, there are other structural options. The case of Caritas Communities illustrates another alternative. Although each of these cases addresses a different issue within the health and human service arena, they are similar in the considerable degree to which the alliances are formally arranged and the corresponding level of integration participation in the alliance yields for the member organizations.

Case Study:	**Caritas Communities, a joint venture**
Reporters:	**Catholic Charities Housing Opportunities &**
	Humility of Mary Housing, Inc.

—OVERVIEW

Caritas Communities is a nonprofit joint venture between Catholic Charities Housing Opportunities (CCHO) and Humility of Mary Housing, Inc. (HMHI) that was formed to manage a 154-unit low-income housing complex in Youngstown, Ohio. The alliance began as a structure through which the member organizations could purchase and manage the property, which was then in foreclosure. As a consequence of tax laws particular to low-income housing development, the joint venture does not own the property outright. Instead, the joint venture entity entered into a separate limited partnership to own and manage the project. This collaborative endeavor provided the members with the needed resource base to undertake a project neither could do on its own.

—PRECONDITIONS

In the spring of 1996, an area legal services association notified CCHO and HMHI that a 154-unit low-income housing complex in Youngstown was in foreclosure. The Department of Housing and Urban Development (HUD), the mortgagor, informed the City of Youngstown that if it could find a nonprofit organization interested in acquiring the property, a special purchase agreement would be arranged.

CCHO, HMHI, and a number of other nonprofit organizations specializing in housing, economic development, and related services attended a
community meeting to review the HUD proposal and meet with residents of
the housing complex. The units were generally well kept, although they
were showing signs of disrepair expected in a 40-year-old property. The
residents were anxious to remain in their homes and excited but cautious
about the prospect of new complex ownership. The energy and commitment of the residents, coupled with the reasonable condition of the infrastructure, led the organizations present at the meeting to agree that the
housing complex needed to be preserved.

HMHI and CCHO, both Catholic housing organizations, expressed interest in participating in the acquisition and preservation efforts but determined that neither could do so alone. HMHI is a nonprofit corporation
sponsored by the Sisters of the Humility of Mary. It provides affordable
housing and supportive services to individuals and families throughout
northeast Ohio. HMHI had the technical expertise to execute the initiative
but was based in an adjacent county and therefore lacked the organizational
credibility and knowledge of the community needed to undertake such a
complex community initiative.

CCHO is the housing and development branch of Catholic Charities of
the Diocese of Youngstown. Based in Youngstown, it serves six counties in
northeast Ohio, providing housing counseling services, development of
low-income housing units, and technical assistance for housing services.
CCHO had strong linkages to the community and a demonstrated history of
successfully addressing housing-related concerns, but it lacked the full
complement of resources to implement such a large-scale project.

CCHO and HMHI had similar missions and values. They were aware of
each other's presence in the community and familiar with each other's services. An administrator from HMHI served on the board of CCHO, and
both organizations were represented on the board of a Youngstown-based
community development corporation. However, the organizations had not
partnered before in a collaborative initiative.

—*PROCESS*

Once the decision to preserve the housing complex was made, CCHO
and HMHI met with city officials and a legal services association to determine how to proceed. They discussed the benefits of partnership, identifying efficiencies of scale, increased service delivery options, and greater
access to resources. These factors were considered significant enough to
merit pursuing an alliance.

Along with getting board approval, one of the first steps in the alliance-
building process for organizations affiliated with the Catholic Diocese was

to obtain the sanction of the local bishop. Once CCHO and HMHI secured this approval, their boards and executives began the alliance structuring process.

The members chose to form a joint venture because they saw it as the best means of incorporating the power and resources of both organizations to accomplish the goal. It was deemed the most appropriate model to ensure equality for both organizations in project ownership. Furthermore, it enabled them to engage in other projects together while shielding each member from the other's liabilities. In July 1996, CCHO and HMHI filed articles of incorporation for the joint venture and applied to the State of Ohio for nonprofit status, thus creating Caritas Communities.

The joint venture was formalized through the establishment of the legally incorporated Caritas Communities. The two members of the joint venture, CCHO and HMHI, have several reserved approval powers relative to Caritas Communities, but governance of the joint venture is vested with the Caritas Communities' board of trustees. The members have limited authority to oversee the board. They review the budget and approve board members; mergers or dissolution; and changes in philosophy or mission, articles of incorporation, and bylaws.

Caritas Communities, the joint venture, is governed by a board of trustees composed of up to 15 organizational member representatives, technical experts, community members, and residents of the complex. Board members serve 3-year, staggered terms. The presidents of CCHO and HMHI serve as chair of the board and president of Caritas Communities, respectively, although the choice of which organization served in which capacity was more arbitrary than it was reflective of the power of one organization in relation to the other in the joint venture.

One of the first issues that the alliance faced was financing. HUD agreed to sell the property to Caritas Communities for $1 in exchange for compliance with three stipulations. First, the complex was to remain a low-income property for 40 years. Second, rents for 64 complex residents, whose incomes were deemed to be too far below the poverty level, were to be frozen for 2 years after the change in possession of the property. These two requirements were consistent with the mission of the joint venture and its member organizations. Consequently, they were accepted.

The third stipulation, and the one that posed a significant challenge in formalizing the purchase agreement, was that a minimum of $2.8 million be invested in rehabilitation. The renovation costs were based on an independent architect's assessment, and although the members concurred that the investment was necessary, their combined resources did not provide for sufficient leverage to fund this aspect of the project. Consequently, the alliance sought technical assistance from a local community development corporation in exploring financing possibilities. By appointing a representative from the development corporation to the Caritas Communities board, the alliance was able to obtain the assistance at no charge.

The alliance secured a loan commitment from an area bank for approximately $700,000, which, although helpful, was not enough to proceed with the deal. After research on alternative financing options excluded the possibility of a bond issue, the only remaining course was to apply for federal and state low-income housing tax credits. Obtaining the tax credits presented two challenges. First, the alliance needed assistance in preparing the tax credit proposal. This issue was readily addressed when a statewide housing capital corporation, with whom alliance members had an established relationship, agreed to write the proposal and incorporate the preparation fee into the financing request.

The second challenge was more complex. Application guidelines mandated that for the alliance to obtain the tax credit, it must have possession of the complex. However, according to HUD's specifications, the alliance could not get possession of the complex unless it could ensure the investment of $2.8 million in renovations. With the support of city, state, and federal agencies and the counsel of numerous attorneys, the alliance used a newly enacted, nonjudicial foreclosure law intended to expedite foreclosures to successfully negotiate the finalization of the deal. The project qualified for the tax credits in early September 1996, and Caritas Communities obtained ownership of the building in late October.

To reap the benefits of the tax credits, which are of no use to charitable, tax-exempt organizations, and to raise the capital needed for the project, low-income housing projects are often undertaken by forming a limited partnership.[1] Taxable limited partners put cash into the partnership and make use of the tax credits. The tax-exempt partner maintains control over the project to ensure that the project is operated consistently with the organization's charitable purposes.

In the case of Caritas Communities, three taxable capital and community development organizations are the equity partners, owning 99% of the limited partnership. The exempt general partner is itself a separate general partnership entity, Youngstown Caritas Housing Co. Caritas Communities owns 78% of the general partnership, and a local Catholic social service organization owns the remainder. The executives of HMHI and CCHO are the officers of the general partner. Because of previous experience managing and developing properties, HMHI's president is the president and CEO, responsible for overall operations. The president of CCHO is the corporate secretary and treasurer and deals with the financial and legal issues. The social service organization was selected as the third member of the general partnership because the alliance wanted to incorporate a community service component for the housing complex. In addition, the organization had an existing relationship with CCHO that expedited the process.

Caritas Communities leveraged $5.6 million for the project, $4.2 million of which resulted from the tax credit. The joint venture development process took approximately 1 year.

Caritas Communities, the joint venture project, has no staff. The two member agencies, CCHO and HMHI, contribute the time of four staff members to the project. HMHI staff provide the management services for the property and oversight for development. CCHO staff coordinate social services, resident access, and training for the resident association. Each organization offers distinct nonpersonnel resources to the project. HMHI coordinates marketing to lease the housing units, and CCHO extended a line of credit to the project because of its greater access to cash.

The Caritas Communities board meets bimonthly and, after more than a year of operation, has finalized its mission, which focuses on providing safe and affordable housing and developing healthy neighborhoods. It is debating what its future scope will be. More specifically, the board is considering whether to limit the joint venture to the current project, undertake another housing project, or engage in more comprehensive economic development activities in the neighborhood.

—OUTCOMES

Although the alliance has not conducted a formal evaluation of the joint venture, members consider the Caritas Communities alliance a success. It achieved its desired outcomes by preserving the 154-unit housing complex, which it currently manages through the nonprofit joint venture. It accomplished this by securing the capital and commitment of the member organizations' boards and staff; private investors; and numerous local, state, and federal agencies to make the project work.

The alliance credits its connection with the Catholic Diocese; the existing relationship between the presidents of CCHO and HMHI; and the organizations' shared vision, mission, and values as factors in the success of the alliance process. All three factors contributed to enhancing critically needed legitimacy and trust within and beyond the alliance. The Catholic Diocese's positive reputation with external stakeholders, including the city, and its collective investments in area banks were influential in expediting negotiations and agreements. Similarly, the previously established relationship between the member organizations allowed them to forgo a lengthy trust-building process. This promoted quick, effective communication and facilitated role clarification as the project moved toward implementation. Both of these factors remain critical in the management of the property.

—REPORTERS' REFLECTIONS AND LESSONS LEARNED

As a result of their participation in the Caritas Communities joint venture, the members were able to identify three fundamental elements of strategic alliance development: (a) Trust in a partner is crucial; (b) members need to share a vision, goals, *and* values before proceeding with such an alliance; and (c) members need to clarify roles and responsibilities up front, so that their expectations of one another are jointly understood. With these things in place, the alliance will have a much stronger foundation on which to continue its development.

PRELIMINARY ANALYSIS: SOME THOUGHTS ON DEVELOPMENT

Theoretical Perspectives

Several theoretical perspectives underlying alliance formation are particularly evident in the analysis of Caritas Communities. The formation of an alliance to preserve the housing complex and maintain the homes of its residents can be viewed easily from the perspective of social responsibility. The decision to proceed was made at a public meeting at the urging of community members and was supported by many organizational stakeholders. The choice by CCHO and HMHI to pursue the alliance was made partly in response to these public expectations and from the perspective of what was best for the community.

The creation of a joint venture between CCHO and HMHI also involved an emphasis on the goals of operational efficiency and resource interdependence. The organizations were interested in pursuing the housing project, but both recognized that the scale of the project meant that neither could do so alone. Individually, the organizations lacked the complete range of resources—including, but not limited to, funding—needed to undertake the project. By collaborating through a joint venture, the members would have a broader resource base from which to undertake the project, and they would be able to use their resources more efficiently in the process.

The missions of the organizations were compatible, but each had a different area of expertise. Together, they could share in the effort of implementing the program, and each member could contribute resources to the project that corresponded with its organizational strengths. In this way, they would be minimizing capacity development costs and maximizing economies of scale. The division of leadership and tasks in the alliance supported this goal.

For HMHI, there was also a need for environmental validity because, although it had experience in property management, the organization was based in a separate county outside of the immediate community. Aligning with CCHO, an organization based in Youngstown, where the property was located, increased HMHI's credibility with the institutions in that community and better positioned it to implement this community redevelopment project effectively.

Alliance Model

The choice of the joint venture model was a critical one. The stipulations of the HUD purchase agreement, as well as the ongoing management of the 154-unit housing complex, presented substantial risk for the alliance members. The structure of the alliance needed to be formal enough to allow for shared responsibility of the project. However, CCHO and HMHI also wanted to maintain their own identities and operations without co-mingling organizational liabilities on other projects. By selecting the joint venture model, both organizations could be more insulated from the project risks.

The choice of the joint venture model allowed the members to create a formalized structure through which they were both able to maintain their equality as partners. The presidents of both member organizations served on the Caritas Communities board, and each serves as an officer in the partnership entity that serves as general partner of Youngstown Caritas Housing Co. The division of roles in this way supports a more equitable balance in power and minimizes conflicts about control of the alliance.

Phases of Development

The assembling phase of the joint venture's development began at the community meeting held to discuss HUD's proposal for the apartment complex. The strong opinions of the community residents and local organizations that the apartment building needed to be preserved, combined with the recognition that the project was too large for any one organization to attempt on its own, provided the impetus to begin alliance development. The community meeting also allowed multiple constituencies to voice their issues and concerns as well as to identify what each was willing to do to support the process. CCHO and HMHI emerged from this meeting as potential partners in the process. Input from the community at this formative stage was an important ingredient in securing stakeholder backing for the project and for the development of the alliance. The next step in the assembling phase was to begin to identify the financial and legal ramifications of undertaking a project of this magnitude. It was at this point, very early in the process, that the organizations first sought expert counsel to develop a deeper understanding of these issues. They met not only with city experts but also with a legal organization to explore these issues. Deciding to proceed, they then obtained approval for the project from their respective boards and the local bishop. The fact that both organizations required the same levels of approval before proceeding likely minimized conflict in the process.

The complex nature of the housing redevelopment project limited the number of structural options from which the partners could choose. The organizations had to have enough accountability to each other to collectively undertake such a large project. However, neither of the organizations wanted to relinquish its autonomy or change the way in which it delivered other services as a result of the partnership. Involving legal counsel early in the process helped the members select the most appropriate alternative and move forward with structuring the alliance quickly.

The ordering phase of this alliance had a particular focus on the management of legal issues. Some of this work is consistent with the development of the joint venture: developing bylaws and filing articles of incorporation and an application for tax-exempt status to establish the joint venture as an independent, nonprofit organization. Yet some of the other aspects of this process related more to the particular technicalities of financing low-income housing redevelopment, including filing for tax credits and establishing the corresponding partnerships in which to use them. However, again, the partners were strategic in how they approached this work, establishing linkages with a community development corporation and a housing capital corporation with specific expertise in these areas to assist in the process.

The issue of trust was a salient one in this case. Although HMHI and CCHO had not collaborated on a project prior to the formation of the joint venture, the organizations' presidents had a positive, existing relationship established through other efforts in the community, including serving on the board of the same organization. In addition, both organizations were associated with the Catholic Diocese and, as such, shared a core set of values. The combination of these two factors provided a foundation of trust between the two organizations. Trust was enhanced in the alliance through open and ongoing communication. The presidents of CCHO and HMHI were available to each other as needed and generally speak with each other regularly. This trusting relationship has been a critical element in creating and maintaining shared power within the alliance.

NOTE

1. For more information about low-income housing tax credits, contact the National Council of State Housing Agencies at http://www.ncsha.org/NCSHA/stateHFA/LIHTC. html.

Part V

COADUNATION

When One New Organization Makes More Sense

Changing circumstances or environmental pressures may prompt organizations to consider an even more radical process of working together known as *coadunation*. Coadunation has also been called strategic restructuring (La Piana, 1997) and involves the combination of two or more organizations into a single organization. Mergers and consolidations are the best known examples.

Placed in the framework at the most formal end of the strategic alliance processes, coadunation traditionally has not been thought of as being a part of the continuum of strategic alliances. Indeed, the complete integration of two or more organizations has been seen as transcending strategic alignment because the focus of such activities is to "materially change the character and locus of control" of the organization (La Piana, 1997, p. 7). When organizations think of coadunation, they often conjure up images of a large organization charging in and taking over a smaller, less powerful one. The perception is more frequently one of acquisition rather than partnership.

But as HSOs plan how they are going to respond to the demands of an increasingly turbulent environment, many are looking to coadunation as the best alternative. Whereas some view it solely from a perspective of loss—lost autonomy, lost identity, lost existence—others see coadunation as opening up a wider range of possibilities for how organizations can maintain the survival of their programs, continue to employ their staff, and preserve their missions on behalf of the com-

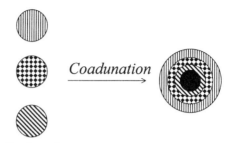

Figure P5.1. Coadunation

munity. In fact, HSOs are entering into the coadunation process to partner with other agencies with compatible values and needs.

Coadunation (from the Latin for "to combine") is the process of strategic interorganizational reorganization that unites two or more organizations within one integrated structure (see Figure P5.1). Its most salient feature is the change in organizational control that accompanies it, because at least one of the partner organizations relinquishes both its autonomy and its identity in the coadunation process. Indeed, the ability of organizations to relinquish autonomy is central to the success of the coadunated alliance. This, in turn, is dependent on the ability of member organizations to see the greater good to be achieved through the process. The core value associated with participation in a coadunated alliance is *self-interests as other interests;* in other words, seeing how one's own goals can best be fulfilled through blending them with the goals of another.

The purpose and strategies of such an alliance must therefore be both organization- and alliance-based. They focus on creating organizational synergies or efficiencies through the process of uniting the two or more partners. As a result, coadunated alliances tend to have few environmental linkages. However, one of these linkages is frequently a major funder, acting as an influential stakeholder, in the decision to coadunate.

Coadunation is also different from the other strategic alliance processes in another important way: The transformation brought about by the alliance is itself a goal of the alliance. A coadunated alliance typically begins with an exploration process, which may be formal or informal. Through this process, alliance members assess the benefits and risks of proceeding. If the organizations do not see a good fit, the alliance may disband, but once a coadunated alliance has moved into the implementation phase, its anticipated duration is permanent.

Organizations that decide to merge or consolidate their operations are faced with the challenge of integrating all aspects of the member organizations—staff, programs, funding, facilities, management information and other systems—including, ultimately, the organizational cultures. Consequently, coadunation is the most structurally complex of the strategic alliance processes. It requires the greatest amount of risk taking on the part of the members and necessitates a tremendous amount of trust on all sides.

Moreover, coadunation is the most emotionally evocative strategic alliance process. An often unstated, yet implicit, aspect of coadunation is recognizing and reconciling the reality of organizational death. Whether a merger, consolidation, or acquisition (to be discussed below), in coadunation the unique life energy that has been the hallmark of each organization now has to be transformed. Amidst possible emotions of anger, depression, and guilt, the primary task in organizational death is to seek closure (Bailey & Grochau, 1993). The process of celebrating what the organizations were, while acknowledging the loss, provides for closure and assists all organizational leaders and members alike in embracing the new possibilities.

Among HSOs, compatibility of mission and culture is usually a big factor in the ease or success with which a coadunated effort takes place. Integrating distinct organizational missions and cultures can be a significant strain on the alliance as it proceeds through its evolution, but legal, financial, or other matters resulting in potential liability can cause the alliance to disband near the outset.

The process of coadunation is extremely formal. Legal contracts and other statutory requirements define the relationship; consequently, legal and other professional assistance plays an important role in the coadunation process.

The role of the board is also critical. As its governing body, the board has legal and fiduciary responsibilities for the HSO. Because coadunation, by definition, requires that at least one member organization be dissolved when the alliance is finalized—ceding its statutory incorporation to the new or remaining organization, which will assume legal and fiduciary responsibility for the combined entity—only the boards of the participating nonprofit organizations can take these governance actions. In some states, nonprofit corporation statutes require approval by the members of a membership organization as well.

The administrative staff of the participating organizations, especially their executive directors and other top management personnel, may be involved on planning committees, but their real role begins with implementation of the agreement as they manage the restructuring process. External facilitators are sometimes brought in as neutral third parties to help move the alliance forward. This can occur at the beginning, middle, and/or end of the process.

Initially, the governance, leadership, and staffing of coadunated alliances resemble those of less formal alliances, where the organizations work side by side to explore the alliance process. However, as the alliance moves toward implementation, activities center increasingly on the integration or blending of the organizational structures. At this time, governance must be unified, leadership and staff fully integrated, and systems such as resource allocation and decision making combined until the organizational members of the new alliance have become fully interdependent and created synergies through their merged operations.

Because of the complexity and formalization inherent in the coadunation process, such alliances often involve a more limited number of organizational partners than do less formal alliances. Interorganizational contact is extensive as organizational members seek to identify and optimize potential synergies across the eight alliance components.

Chapter 10

MERGERS, CONSOLIDATIONS, AND ACQUISITIONS

Mergers and consolidations are two of the most familiar models of co-adunated alliances. *Mergers* are legally sanctioned alliances in which one or more organizations dissolve and are absorbed by another. The surviving organization retains the assets and liabilities of both organizations. *Consolidations* are statutorily defined alliances in which two or more organizations are fully dissolved, and one newly incorporated organization is created. The assets and liabilities of the organizations are combined and belong to this new organization, and one new governing board is formed.

As with any newly formed nonprofit organization, a consolidated organization must comply with all statutory and Internal Revenue Service (IRS) application procedures in order to incorporate and receive tax-exempt status. In a merger, because the dissolved organization is transferring its assets and liabilities to an existing organization, the legal steps concerned may be different. In either case, the transaction leads to a major structural redefinition of participating organizations and therefore requires the involvement of legal counsel beginning in the earliest stages.

State nonprofit corporation statutes may impose very specific procedural requirements on these kinds of transactions. In addition, depending on the nature of the reorganization and the regulatory style of the state's attorney general, early consultation with that office may be useful, or even essential. Participating organizations may also need to seek private letter rulings from the IRS *in advance* of the transaction in order to have assurance that the contemplated changes will not have adverse tax consequences for the organizations.

Consider the example of the voluntary merger between the Center for Abuse Prevention, Inc. (referred to hereafter as the Center) and Northwestern Ohio Treatment and Crisis Line, Inc. (NOTCL), where the Center was the surviving organization. The Center served a four-county area through abuse prevention programs in schools, treatment programs, court advocacy, and community education. NOTCL was known for its domestic violence work. It operated a women's shelter, provided court advocacy, and ran a domestic violence intervention program for a five-county area.

At the time of merger consideration, the Center had been in business for 14 years, with its service niche of primarily child sexual abuse treatment for adults and children. However, two years earlier, the Center expanded its mission to include prevention and treatment for all types of abuse, including domestic violence. About the same time, other organizations, including some for-profits, began competing with the Center for its traditional service niche. Consequently, the Center wanted to gain power to overcome the competition and to be recognized for its range of abuse prevention and treatment programs.

NOTCL had credibility as a provider of domestic violence prevention and treatment programs and had a particularly strong presence in the county in which the Center was the weakest. In addition, the organization had numerous funding sources and a large cash reserve, whereas the Center historically had cash flow problems because of its heavy reliance on insurance reimbursements and client fees.

When the executive of NOTCL left the organization, one of its board members, who also served on the Center's board, called the Center's executive to help generate ideas of who in the community might fill the vacant director position. The Center's executive suggested the idea of forming an alliance between the two organizations. The board member, knowing a lot about the two organizations, thought the idea was a good one.

Both boards approved the idea, and the two organizations jointly hired an attorney to facilitate the process. From the outset, the organizations pursued the idea of a merger. The attorney worked extensively with both boards as he conducted due diligence and prepared the paperwork to formalize the merger. All information was disseminated through the board meetings and other forms of verbal communication, and decisions were made by majority rule of the joint boards. There was minimal conflict between the boards because of their shared values and goals. Moreover, when NOTCL finally hired an interim director, it hired an administrator from the Center on a contract basis, so the organizations' directors were working toward common goals.

Merging NOTCL with the Center took about 6 months. The merged organization retained the Center's name, and, as part of the process, two of the NOTCL board members joined the Center's board. NOTCL had requested that the Center keep as many of its employees as possible. At the time of the merger, each organization had eight employees, all of whom were retained in the process.

Overall, NOTCL lost its identity as a result of the merger, but all of its services were maintained, and its staff gained in both improved pay and benefits. The combined organization had more power in the counties in which each had previously been weak, and the Center stabilized its financial position.

Whereas merger and consolidation represent two models of coadunated alliances, there is a third: *acquisition.* Often, when "acquisition" is used to describe coadunations among HSOs, these alliances actually fit this chapter's definition of merger. In such situations, the term is used to emphasize an unequal relationship between the merging organizations. The choice of the term frequently implies a significant size or power differential among the participants (La Piana, 1997).

The use of the term acquisition is additionally misleading because, unlike for-profit corporations, nonprofit organizations do not typically issue shares representing organizational ownership. Therefore, this model works differently in the context of nonprofits than in the for-profit context, where acquisition involves transfer (commonly through purchase) of the acquired company's stock to the acquiring company. However, beyond the implication that an acquisition is a merger of unequal partners, another way that one nonprofit organization may acquire another is through a restructuring agreement, in which control of the acquired organization's board membership is ceded to the acquiring organization, thus integrating the organizations at the governance level.

Such an acquisition took place between Planned Parenthood Mar Monte (PPMM) and East Valley Community Clinic (EVCC) in Santa Clara County, California. Through the acquisition, EVCC became a subsidiary of PPMM but continued to exist as a separately incorporated local section 501(c)(3) organization with its own board. However, its organizational bylaws were changed to state that the organization was a wholly owned subsidiary of PPMM, and all of the EVCC board members were approved by the PPMM board. The EVCC board president and several other EVCC board members served on the PPMM board. In addition, PPMM provided all administrative and management services for EVCC through a management contract.

The acquisition model was chosen to create EVCC as a subsidiary of PPMM because it allowed EVCC to keep its identity and its current funding streams, some of which would have been difficult for PPMM to secure and maintain. PPMM credits its ability to identify this structural arrangement as the most advantageous to the fact that it had been involved in eight other mergers and strategic alliances prior to pursuing this partnership.

Regardless of how many times an HSO has engaged in previous strategic alliances or whether an acquisition involves a restructuring agreement (or is, in fact, a merger), advice of legal counsel is strongly encouraged to ensure conformity with state regulations and to avoid unintended tax ramifications to the alliance members. Similarly, the legal requirements for each of these three coadunated structures vary and need to be considered relative to the overall goals and expectations of the member organizations.

The following case study presents a scenario in which four organizations determined that each would be best served through a consolidation rather than a merger or acquisition. In this case study, all four members relinquished their identities in favor of a newly incorporated nonprofit organization largely to maintain the equity among the partners.

Case Study:	**Arbor Circle, a consolidation**
Reporter:	**Child Guidance/Arbor Circle**

—OVERVIEW

The creation of Arbor Circle was the result of the consolidation of four HSOs in Grand Rapids, Michigan. The growing impact of managed care on the service domain of these organizations, coupled with the increasing competition for clients and funding among nonprofit organizations, was threatening the survival of the four community-based organizations. The organizations were also faced with the challenge of responding to how structural changes within state agencies would affect them individually and how they could limit the impact of these changes on them organizationally through the development of an alliance. The coadunation process allowed the member organizations to establish a continuum of care that more strongly positioned them to respond to these issues. Shared leadership, the active involvement of staff, and the fact that turf protection did not become a major issue permitted the alliance to proceed successfully, although the full integration of the distinct organizational cultures has continued to present challenges for the new organization.

—PRECONDITIONS

The driving forces for the Arbor Circle alliance centered on the environmental changes taking place in the behavioral and mental health domains of the nonprofit sector in the mid-1990s. Child Guidance, a behavioral health provider, and other area service providers were aware that the complexities brought about by the requirements of managed care posed significant challenges for individual nonprofit organizations providing targeted services to a focused consumer population. Moreover, the State of Michigan had reorganized the Department of Social Services and merged the departments of Mental Health and Public Health, necessitating adjustments in the service provision practices of Michigan's community organizations.

In the fall of 1994, the executive director of Child Guidance convened a meeting with the executive directors of two local HSOs providing a complementary array of services: the Advisory Center for Teens and Family Impact. Child Guidance, which offered multiple programs for preadolescent children, had recently secured a contract to manage Mercy Respite Center, a residential facility for children and adolescents with developmental disorders. So, at the time of the meeting, Child Guidance's executive director was serving as the director of Mercy Respite Center as well. The Advisory Center for Teens, located near Child Guidance, programmatically picked up where Child Guidance left off, providing services to youth from adolescence into their early 20s. Family Impact was a single-program, single-funder mental health agency serving families with children at risk for out-of-home placement. Together, the members represented a regional service area. They all served the local metropolitan area but also provided services in several neighboring counties.

The three executives met to discuss the impact of the recent local and federal reforms on their organizations. The discussion led the organizations to collectively conduct an environmental scan, which resulted in more conversations about the environmental impact on service provision. The executives collectively considered how the changes would affect their organizations and how the effects might be mitigated by the creation of an alliance.

Prior to the move toward managed care, competition among the four organizations had been limited. In fact, they had positive prior working relationships. However, external pressures from funders and other institutional stakeholders were driving the need of these and other community organizations to maximize effectiveness with even more emphasis on efficiency. Funding competition was coupled with the perception that organizations now needed to achieve a critical service mass to protect their organizational and consumer interests. Child Guidance and its potential partners experienced this issue as the need to be strong enough organizationally to survive in this rapidly changing environment.

—PROCESS

Alliance building began in the fall of 1994 with the meeting of the potential partners convened by the executive at Child Guidance. Because the organizations, and their executives, were familiar with one another, minimal time had to be spent on member identification in the alliance development process.

In choosing potential partners, Child Guidance considered the organizational vision of each agency, its ability to cope with constant change, and its commitment to a compatible mission of serving the community. The selected member organizations were all mission-oriented, community-based nonprofits that recognized the need to operate differently if they were going to survive, given the scope and pace of the changes in the behavioral health field. Their executives saw the opportunity, through the formation of an alliance, to provide a continuum of services in an increasingly competitive service arena. They acknowledged that while an alliance would mean a loss of autonomy for them, the benefits, including the ability to reduce overhead and redirect resources, would actually make them more viable. The overall purpose of the alliance, however, was organizational survival.

Next, the organizations jointly facilitated a 3-day retreat with the administrative staffs of their organizations. The purpose of the retreat was to conduct an environmental scan and begin strategic planning. The results of the scan supplied the momentum to proceed with collective action. From the beginning, the executive directors of the partnering organizations served as equal partners. Whereas the alliance members shared leadership of the alliance, the Child Guidance executive served as the facilitator to keep the process moving forward.

Following the fall retreat, members created three teams to explore issues and coordinate the tasks associated with the alliance development process. These teams involved staff, administrators, and board members in the alliance process. A clinical design team was appointed to examine member services and recommend ways in which to link them. The team consisted of clinical staff representing the four programmatic entities: Child Guidance, Advisory Center for Teens, Family Impact, and Mercy Respite Center. A governance team, comprised of administrative staff, was assembled to evaluate structural options for the alliance. The third team was the board transition committee. The committee was made up of three trustees from each of the member organizations. Its purpose was threefold: facilitate the development of relationships among the members of the four boards; assist the boards in becoming familiar with the other organizations; and, based on the selected alliance structure, oversee the transition of the four boards, which together had 60 members. The governance and clinical design teams reported to the board transition committee.

The three executives divided responsibilities for the committees. The executive of Family Impact participated on the clinical committee. The other two executives were active on the governance committee, and all three staffed the board transition committee.

The members considered various types of alliances, from a loose affiliation to a merger, in making their decisions about structure. However, in the course of exploring ways in which they could link their services, the clinical design team identified the merger structure as one that would best support what the members wanted to accomplish programmatically. The governance team, which had been expected initially to select the alliance structure, expanded on the work of the clinical design team and began focusing specifically on a merger in March 1995.

Later that spring, the board transition committee hosted a meeting of the board members from all of the partner organizations. The retreat was facilitated by the former executive of a large and influential local human service organization. It was held in the highest building in the city. The facilitator and location were selected purposefully to encourage visionary thinking among the board members during the process. This meeting marked the turning point at which the process moved from an exploratory affiliation to the serious consideration of a merger.

Once the structure was identified, systematic work began toward implementing the alliance. To maximize its success, and in keeping with the equality of all partners in the process, the members agreed that each organization would be dissolved, and a newly incorporated nonprofit organization with a new name and a new board would be created to integrate their programs and services. The members called the alliance a merger, but, by definition, this restructuring classified the Arbor Circle alliance as a consolidation rather than a merger.

Once the decision to consolidate was made, the members conducted due diligence to learn more about each other's organizations. As in most due diligence investigations, the legal staff and the executives reviewed each other's human resource and financial systems, as well as any potential legal liabilities the members might have that would carry over into the consolidation. The due diligence team reported its findings to the board transition committee. Due diligence continued through October 1995, taking about 3 months.

At the same time, members were negotiating the formal and legal issues necessary to dissolve each of the organizations and create a new nonprofit entity. This included creating new articles of incorporation and bylaws as well as securing tax-exempt status for the new organization. The legal staffs from the member organizations were largely responsible for this work.

Communication with internal and external stakeholders was a central focus during the alliance development process. The member organizations were purposeful about keeping staff involved in the process through staff meetings and other forums. The organizations' executives talked a lot with staff about their roles and how these roles would change after the consolidation. Restructuring was a part of the consolidation plan, and one important role for the executives of the member organizations was reassuring staff that no mass layoffs would result. Additional training would be required of some staff, but organizational leaders were committed to reducing overhead through attrition, a commitment they adhered to following the consolidation.

The executives sought to encourage participatory management, attempting to keep decisions pushed out to the areas where they were the most relevant. This meant that considerable time was spent with management and staff processing specific issues. Moreover, the leaders tried to provide sufficient opportunities for all levels of staff to discuss their issues and concerns.

The alliance leadership also made concerted efforts to keep external stakeholders informed throughout the process. The executives visited funders, payors, and business and community groups to explain the consolidation plan. Most groups were supportive of the plan. However, one funder was vocal in its concerns about the potential negative impact of the consolidation. The funder felt that the alliance would limit service choices. This concern has been alleviated with time as Arbor Circle has continued to offer high-quality services to consumers.

Early discussions about decision making, emphasizing the egalitarian relationship among the members, helped minimize conflict. Similarly, the decision to begin the new structure with four divisions (not unlike the four consolidating members) and gradually move to two divisions (i.e., behavioral health and prevention services) to accommodate the 23 programs also helped reduce tension and conflict during the process.

The member organizations set January 1, 1996, as the goal for finalizing the consolidation. To ease the transition, this date was selected because it corresponded with the beginning of the fiscal year for each of the member organizations. However, from the outset, the executives had emphasized to staff and other stakeholders that all decisions on how to integrate the organizations would not be complete by the formal consolidation date. The complete integration of the member organizations into a unified Arbor Circle would take considerably more time and would require the participation of employees to make the transition successful.

The consolidation occurred within the projected timeline. In October 1995, the boards of each of the member organizations passed a resolution declaring that, effective January 1, 1996, their organizations would cease to exist in favor of Arbor Circle, and on January 1, 1996, Arbor Circle began operating. The executive director of Child Guidance became the president of Arbor Circle. One of the executives assumed the position of Vice President and Chief Operating Officer, and the other resigned to pursue other career opportunities. The decisions regarding executive leadership of the new organization were made jointly by the three executives based on their career goals and professional interests.

—OUTCOMES

The consolidation was formally completed on January 1, 1996. The alliance chose to evaluate its success by assessing its progress in three main areas: the support it received from the community and consumers, integration of program services, and the creation of a new corporate culture. The alliance's executives consider it a success but admit that fully measuring success is ongoing as the consolidation development process continues.

The community supports the organization, although some of the expected outcomes have not materialized completely. Benchmarks of stakeholder support include an increase in contracts and a 23% increase in the organizational allocation from United Way in the first year of operations. However, cost savings have been delayed. One reason is that Arbor Circle has honored its pledge to its employees to handle overhead reduction through attrition. Despite reducing short-term savings, organizational leaders believe that this approach has resulted in building a much stronger organizational foundation from which Arbor Circle will benefit in the long term.

Many of the anticipated positive effects of the consolidation on service integration have been realized. Arbor Circle provides a continuum of services and has created economies of scale in the provision of these services that give the organization more power in the community. This increase in power has resulted in greater efficacy of the organization's advocacy efforts on behalf of its consumers. Yet again, executives admit that the integration of services is a long process.

The Arbor Circle leaders underestimated the amount of work that would be required to integrate the distinct cultures of four organizations into one organization with 240 employees. Each organization had different connections to the communities, and internal dynamics. Arbor Circle has been challenged as it has tried to balance the continuation of certain features from each of the member organizations and the creation of new organizational strategies, systems, and tasks to yield the maximum benefit for its consumers.

The organization held a retreat in 1996 to facilitate the integration process with staff. The issues and concerns raised at the retreat solidified staff around the integration process. People made commitments to each other and have honored them. Moreover, none of the employees or board members placed turf issues above the mission of the organization and the best interests of its consumers. The executives of Arbor Circle see this as one of the principle reasons for the consolidation's success. However, they acknowledge in retrospect that the process would have been strengthened further if they had allowed for greater input of consumers in the planning stage.

Given the size of similar organizations in the area, Arbor Circle executives consider it a mid-sized organization. They see the new organization's size as yielding both benefits and costs. Its size is a positive feature because it allows the organization to better leverage its resources. At the same time, it may be too small to take advantage of some opportunities and too large to engage effectively in others. Moreover, with regard to internal systems, the executive management team is less connected to what happens in the organization on a daily basis. This means that they need to rely more on middle managers to get information, rather than being directly involved, as they were before the organizations consolidated.

One further outcome from the alliance process was the subsequent merger of Arbor Circle with a local substance abuse program. In much the same way as the selection of the initial partners had been done, the addition of the substance abuse program to Arbor Circle's continuum of services was based on the findings from the 1994 environmental scan, in this case identifying substance abuse as a potential gap in services. Discussions with the program began early in 1997, and the merger was completed October 1, 1997. This merger allowed Arbor Circle to further diversify its programs and services.

—REPORTER'S REFLECTIONS AND LESSONS LEARNED

In addition to realizing that the success of the alliance must continue to be demonstrated over the long term, Arbor Circle learned several other lessons as a result of the consolidation. First, communication is an essential element of an effective coadunation process. The executives and board members of the participating organizations need to share information with each other. However, communication with other stakeholders is also important. This means that the organizational leaders need to make their staffs and community stakeholders aware of the process and need to take responsibility for keeping them informed on a regular basis about what is happening.

Another equally important lesson that the Arbor Circle executives learned was that combining diverse organizations creates power. Yet a critical element in the realization of this power is paying sufficient attention to existing organizational cultures and working to integrate them in a way that honors them and, at the same time, places the overall mission and vision for the community first.

PRELIMINARY ANALYSIS:
SOME THOUGHTS ON DEVELOPMENT

Theoretical Perspectives

A central motivator for the Arbor Circle consolidation was the desire for strategic enhancement. Survival was cited as the overriding purpose of the alliance and central to the rationale for participation among all members. The organizations were beginning to see the effects of managed care and agency restructuring throughout the state. They felt that in order to respond to what they experienced as an increasingly competitive marketplace, they needed to be stronger organizationally. Viewed from the strategic enhancement perspective, improving their strategic position was necessary for the organizations to continue offering their services to the community, and creating an alliance was one way to achieve this goal.

The desire of the members to increase their power in the service domain was a related motivator, thus supporting the domain influence perspective of alliance formation. With the changes occurring within the service delivery environment, the participating organizations saw the need to increase their power as a means of organizational survival. The alliance's focus on its success as a stronger advocate for consumers validates the existence of this goal. However, even after consolidating four organizations initially, and then merging with a fifth, Arbor Circle remains a mid-size organization relative to its competitors. Consequently, its executives continue to weigh both the positive and negative features of their size and relative power with the alliance's ability to meet the needs of the community.

Finally, from an operational efficiency perspective, the members were aware that in order to be more competitive in the managed care arena, they needed to create economies of scale and more efficient operating procedures. Arbor Circle has been successful in this area, reducing overheads and redirecting resources. However, the challenge of integrating the structures and systems of first four, and then five, organizations without staff layoffs has made this process and the realization of operational synergies more time-consuming than had been expected.

Alliance Model

The alliance began as an informal affiliation in which four organizations worked together to assess the changing service climate and its potential implications for the delivery of services to their consumers. The members agreed early in the process that the creation of a more formal alliance would improve the sustainability of these programs amid these changes. However, in selecting the consolidation model as the most appropriate alliance option, the process evolved differently from what the alliance leaders had expected.

The recommendation to engage in consolidation emerged from a study of the best way to integrate the organizations' programs. The proposal was submitted by the clinical design team rather than the governance team that was evaluating the structural alternatives. This selection process illustrates the flexibility of the members and emphasizes the priority that the member organizations had placed on the benefits of the alliance for their consumers. The consolidation model was chosen because it provided the most effective way of achieving the organizations' service delivery goals.

The evolution of the alliance demonstrates the interrelatedness of an alliance's components and supports the contention that a comprehensive appraisal of multiple alliance components is important in determining the alliance structure. Had another type of alliance been selected first and the program goals forced to conform to the model, the alliance might not be as successful in accomplishing these goals.

Finally, the Arbor Circle consolidation also reflects the confusion around current terminology discussed throughout this book. Arbor Circle thought of this alliance as a merger. However, according to the definitions provided in this text, it is a consolidation. Arbor Circle was a new nonprofit organization that assumed the assets and liabilities of its four member organizations. The members separately incorporated Arbor Circle prior to the formalization of the consolidation. They applied for tax-exempt status for the new organization and established a new board.

The caution in interchanging the terms "merger" and "consolidation," and losing sight of the distinction between them, is that doing so may cause others inclined to pursue these models to misunderstand or under-estimate the organizational and legal tasks involved in each option.

Phases of Development

The four developmental phases of an alliance are exemplified clearly in the case of Arbor Circle. Assembling centered on the first meetings organized with the members of the four partner organizations and their assessment of the changing service climate. As part of the assembling phase, the organizations engaged in a 3-day retreat to collectively identify the initial costs and benefits associated with pursuing an alliance. The executive at Child Guidance served as the convener of these meetings, but from the beginning, each of the partners was considered equal, and they all shared leadership of the alliance.

Once the decision to form an alliance was made, and committees were structured to begin exploring the process, Arbor Circle moved into the ordering phase of development. In creating the committees, the executives broadened the alliance to include clinical and legal staff and trustees from each of their organizations. Throughout this phase, the committees considered many of the details pertaining to how the organizations would work together, including identifying how services could be integrated and how the alliance could be structured.

Performing began at the joint board retreat when the decision to proceed with the consolidation was made. The committee structure, established in the ordering phase to investigate specific issues, now moved ahead to negotiating them more specifically. Stakeholders at all levels of the organization were involved in operationalizing the consolidation through both individual activities and group work.

The activities in the ordering and performing phases of the alliance's development were strengthened through the input of multiple staff and board perspectives. Structuring the work to incorporate the expertise of staff and board members assisted the alliance in focusing its efforts and enhanced its results. For example, clinical staff largely worked on defining service integration, legal and administrative staff conducted due diligence, and board members implemented the board transition and oversaw the coadunation process. Moreover, keeping staff and community groups informed about what was happening on a regular basis minimized threats to the success of the alliance by increasing their understanding of the process.

The alliance leaders planned a gradual integration of the four organizations into one following the formal consolidation. For example, to achieve maximum synergies, one structural objective for the new organization was to consolidate programs and services into two divisions. However, to ease the impact of this transition on the staff and consumers, this integration was planned in stages. Immediately following the formal consolidation, Arbor Circle's programs and services would be structured in four divisions that resembled the operations of each of the member organizations prior to the consolidation. The integration of these programs and services into two divisions would be conducted over time. As such, the ordering and performing stages will continue until these tasks and other tasks associated with integrating the organizational cultures are complete.

Keeping in mind the iterative and sometimes concurrent nature of these developmental phases, however, the transforming phase began on January 1, 1996, when the consolidation was formalized, and Arbor Circle began operating as one organization rather than an alliance of four separate entities. The focus of this phase, comprehensively evaluating the effort, is ongoing at the same time that Arbor Circle continues to fully integrate the organizational cultures of the member organizations.

A notable feature of this alliance and its development that the members attributed to the consolidation's ultimate success is that the alliance members remained equal partners throughout the process. The members were able to do this because they worked to develop trust among the executives as well as with board members and employees. They attended diligently to the timely dissemination of information among the partnering organizations and at all levels of the organizations throughout the process.

One important aspect of this communication process was the honest estimate that leaders made about how the process would progress. The leaders were clear in their communications with stakeholders that despite the establishment of a formal January 1 consolidation date, the consolidation process would not be complete on that day. Instead, they emphasized the need for all stakeholders to continue to work toward integrating structures, systems, and services effectively. This strategy permitted staff to be more involved in the process, thereby gaining more ownership and commitment to its success. The alliance leaders remain convinced that this approach, although possibly more time consuming, has made the consolidated organization an even stronger one.

Part VI

ALLIANCE EVALUATION

A critical aspect of the creation and maintenance of strategic alliances is evaluating how well that alliance has achieved its stated goals. However, this crucial piece of the process is often overlooked. A national study of strategic alliances revealed that fewer than half (47%) of the organizations surveyed formulated criteria that they could use to assess the effectiveness of the alliance process or its outcomes (Yankey et al., 1999).

The same study illustrated a second issue involving the evaluation of strategic alliances. Despite the acknowledged importance of organizational culture and the interpersonal elements of alliance development, such as trust building and turf protection, the alliance *process* is rarely considered in establishing the evaluation plan. Consequently, when evaluations are implemented in strategic alliance initiatives at all, they tend to center almost solely on the *products* of the alliance. Although the outcomes are important, as witnessed in the case studies described earlier, they tell only part of the story regarding how well the alliance is working.

This concluding chapter thus revisits key points from the preceding chapters, shows how they connect to one another in an actual alliance situation, and explores ways in which this information can be used to evaluate the effectiveness and accountability of strategic alliances. Much can be learned from integrating information about alliance development into evaluations of these partnerships, particularly by using a method known as participatory action research. Because this approach focuses on measuring both qualitative and quantitative change, it is able to reveal things that traditional methods of evaluation often do not. Moreover, because it relies on the active involvement of members of the system being studied in the entire evaluation process, it provides data that can be used to improve not only their products, but also their process.

Chapter 11

STRENGTHENING AN ALLIANCE
THROUGH EVALUATION

Building on the concept of "action research" coined by Kurt Lewin (1946), and integrating the philosophy of Paulo Freire (1970), participatory action research (PAR) brings the system's participants into the evaluation process not at the end, but at the beginning. It involves the sharing of information between evaluators and participants and the co-creation between these groups of the direction and design of the evaluation process (Whyte, 1991). Thus, PAR can provide an information-rich approach to assessing the development and outcomes of a strategic alliance. It enables the alliance to develop an infrastructure for designing and evaluating its own progress as it moves through the successive phases of its growth, and it can provide the alliance with a framework for making such changes as are needed in both its process and the content or focus of its work.

In designing a plan for research, evaluators must address at least four fundamental questions: (a) What is to be evaluated? (b) How will it be evaluated? (c) How will the data be analyzed? and (d) What will be done with the findings? "Research is participatory when those directly affected by it influence each of these four decisions and help carry them out" (Elden, 1987, pp. 257-258).

In evaluating the progress and outcomes of a strategic alliance, the participatory action research method may proceed as follows:

1. *Entry:* Alliance stakeholders and researchers begin a dialogue with the goal of establishing a collaborative relationship for exploring the alliance's issues that will focus on both needs and assets.

2. *Data gathering:* Researchers and selected alliance stakeholders work as a team and systematically gather data through interviews, questionnaires, observations, and other means that they define.

3. *Data analysis and feedback:* The evaluation team of researchers and alliance stakeholders reviews and organizes the data to identify key findings. The team reports these findings to the alliance-at-large so that all of the partners can begin to develop a collective understanding of the emerging data and the issues that they reveal.

4. *Planning and action:* Specific plans of action to resolve issues identified in the data analysis and feedback process are developed and implemented.

5. *Evaluation:* The results of each action are evaluated as additional data, as indicated by discussion, are gathered (Bailey, 1992b).

It should be noted here that, although these five steps can be separated conceptually, the activities in this research process are actually cyclical, overlapping, and iterative, sometimes leading the process to turn back, or build on, itself. For example, the feedback gained from sharing newly gathered data with the partners may lead to the decision to gather more or different data. In this way, the new information gathered from one phase to the next is integrated into the ongoing evaluation process, strengthening it and allowing it to be refined continuously.

Thus, in contrast to traditional methods of evaluation, in which the subjects of the research are often treated paradoxically as objects, the investigators and the alliance partners in participatory action research become what has been termed "co-inquirers" (Wolfe, 1980). Instead of waiting until the end of the alliance process to evaluate its success, and then taking their findings away to use for their own purposes, PAR investigators work in partnership with alliance members to conduct an ongoing evaluation through which they collectively generate findings and use their feedback to refine the evaluation process. The alliance members use the findings and feedback to improve the alliance process, and these improvements are, in turn, evaluated, and so on. Together, researchers and strategic alliance members form what amounts to a co-inquiry team that philosophically and literally embodies the spirit and practice of participatory action research.

Using participatory action research as the basis for planning and conducting the evaluation also allows for the inclusion in the evaluation process of other stakeholders, such as consumers, who have an interest in the alliance and its outcomes. Conducting the evaluation in conjunction with representatives of the alliance and its relevant constituencies not only increases the usefulness of the process, but it also fosters internal ownership of both the process and its outcomes. This is vital because process and outcomes are inextricably linked: The components essential to the creation and maintenance of strategic alliances—leadership, membership, environmental linkages, purpose, tasks, strategies, structure, and systems—are also important for their evaluation.

INTEGRATING EVALUATION WITH STRATEGIC ALLIANCE DEVELOPMENT

Involving alliance stakeholders in the ongoing evaluation process provides data for evaluation, and it gives valuable external, as well as internal, feedback on the successes and failures of the alliance. Likewise, continually revisiting and monitoring each of the alliance's components throughout its evolution not only provides a cumulative flow of data but also allows for continuous program improvement, thus integrating the evaluation process with alliance development. A series of questions may be posed to both strengthen each of the developmental phases and facilitate the transition of the alliance from one phase to the next.[1]

How was the leader identified?

How were members recruited?

How much time was spent in the recruitment process?

How representative is the membership of the alliance with regard to its targeted population and/or its issue domain?

How was the alliance convened?

Do leaders and members share a common understanding of the alliance's purpose?

Are leaders' and members' roles and responsibilities understood?

Are anticipated linkages between the members' parent organizations and the alliance clearly delineated?

In the assembling phase, critical questions that need to be asked concern the process of member recruitment and the role of the leader in establishing a common vision for the alliance.

The alliance's success in moving from the assembling phase into the ordering phase is measured by the effectiveness with which the leadership and members have dealt with other practical issues. Critical questions here focus on these issues.

- Was the development of an appropriate structure initiated to accomplish this purpose (i.e., the organization of the alliance)?
- Have the stakeholders established systems and norms for managing consensus and conflict?
- Are policies and guidelines in place to achieve the alliance's purpose?
- Does the alliance have the appropriate bylaws, contracts, or other agreements in place to govern its relationships and activities?
- How is information to be disseminated to members?
- What systems are in place for the budgeting and distribution of other resources?
- What processes exist to address the issues of membership turnover?
- How will new members be incorporated into the alliance?
- Have informal leaders begun to emerge?
- How are these leaders incorporated into the leadership group (i.e., the formal and informal leaders)?
- What benefits and costs do leaders and members accrue as a result of their participation in the alliance?
- Do the benefits of participation outweigh the costs of membership?

By asking these questions along the way, any remaining challenges are isolated for special attention, allowing the opportunity for continuous improvement.

In transitioning from ordering to performing, the alliance focuses on safeguarding its resources and activities from external interference and strengthening (or rediscovering) its internal validity and creative energy in pursuit of the accomplishment of its purpose. In the performing phase, the stakeholders are actively operationalizing the various systems that have been established (e.g., financial, human resources, and evaluation) and are executing the specific tasks necessary to accomplish the alliance's goals. Key questions to consider at this phase examine the success of the alliance in accomplishing its tasks.

- Do members understand their individual roles in the context of the alliance?
- How successful have members been in putting the goals of the alliance before their own or their organizations' needs?
- How effectively and/or efficiently are the alliance systems (e.g., information dissemination, resource allocation) working?
- Does the leader provide opportunities for members to acknowledge their progress and setbacks?
- How are requirements for additional or different resources identified?
- Are lessons learned used to amend the alliance process?

To move the alliance into the transforming phase, all of the partners (including the researchers) must focus on assessing the outcomes of the alliance's efforts over time, discussing strategies for improvement, and identifying additional community concerns and potential linkages. In the transforming phase itself, as the alliance progresses toward refinement, reformation, or dissolution, the leader and the members assess its process and the content of its activities both formally and informally. Helpful questions here explore the alliance transformation process.

- What factors are precipitating the transformation?
- What was the leader's role in the decision?
- What role did the members have in the decision?
- How was the need to transform the alliance communicated to the rest of the alliance? To its environmental linkages?
- To what extent do the leaders, members, and environmental linkages agree with the decision to transform the alliance?
- To what extent do they feel the purpose of the alliance was fulfilled?

During the performing and transforming phases, questions regarding the specific products or outcomes of what the alliance sought to achieve are also added to the evaluation. Such questions are developed as the evaluation systems are defined in the ordering phase and receive continued emphasis alongside the process questions as the alliance continues.

HOW PAR WORKS IN PRACTICE:
A REAL-LIFE EXAMPLE

The following example is an illustration of the PAR approach as applied to the earlier referenced 6-year evaluation of the Healthy Family/Healthy Start (HF/HS) consortium, a community-based effort to reduce infant mortality and improve birth and health outcomes for women and infants in 16 Cleveland neighborhoods (Bailey, 1992b; Bailey & Koney, 1995b).

This evaluation was both formative—focusing on the process used by the consortium to implement its programs and services—and summative—examining achievement of the desired outcomes. Integrating PAR with the alliance's own development life cycle created an evaluation process that established a mechanism for ongoing feedback between researchers and consortium members through three co-inquiry teams, thus allowing for the continuous improvement of the consortium process at the consumer, staff, and administrative levels. Through their involvement in these teams, consortium members were co-investigators in the evaluation. The teams likewise provided a point of entry through which the evaluators participated in the consortium.

Originally, a single team was envisioned to coordinate the evaluation, but because of the consortium's complex structure, it soon became evident to the evaluators and the consortium members that three co-inquiry teams were needed to ensure comprehensive representation from various levels of the consortium in the evaluation. Similarly, early in the evaluation planning process, member input led to the decision to use existing committees as co-inquiry teams in order to minimize the number of meetings that members would be asked to attend. To the extent possible, attempts were made to combine co-inquiry team activities with regularly scheduled meetings.

These co-inquiry teams were structured to involve subcontractors, community members, and staff in the evaluation. The teams worked with the consortium evaluators in data collection, feedback, and analysis, as well as in action planning for improvement. The committees associated with the co-inquiry teams generally met monthly and frequently discussed issues related to the consortium process and the achievement of goals and objectives. These meetings were central forums for the monitoring and evaluation processes.

Working from the analyzed data, evaluators shared their findings and recommendations with co-inquiry team members to get their feedback and provide for further analysis. Together, the entire team formulated action plans to address targeted issues.

HOW THE EVALUATION PROCESS ACHIEVED ITS GOALS

The overriding goal of the evaluation process was to provide information to strengthen the process of consortium development and thus increase its overall effectiveness and accountability. Effectiveness was defined as the quality of both process and products based on internal and external assessments. It was measured by surveying the degree to which members were satisfied with the quality of the consortium process, the extent to which the consortium met its goals and objectives, and the level of satisfaction that members expressed with goal and objective accomplishment.

Accountability was defined as the consortium's responsiveness to standards and demands (Schopler, 1987). It was measured by surveying the consortium's level of responsiveness to the standards and demands of the grantee, project area residents and consumers, and its members.

The evaluation explored five questions: (a) What process or processes were used by the consortium to implement its programs and services? (b) What were the strengths of the consortium process(es)? (c) What were the weaknesses of the consortium process(es)? (d) How effective was the consortium in achieving its goals and objectives? and (e) How accountable was the consortium in achieving its goals and objectives? These research questions were guided by the requirements of a federal grant, but conversations between the evaluators and consortium members were instrumental in their conceptualization.

To answer these questions, the evaluation used four sources of data: participant and nonparticipant observations of consortium meetings; surveys of consortium members; focus groups; and analyses of consortium records such as meeting minutes, agendas, and memos. Evaluators regularly attended consortium meetings, taking process notes and collecting meeting materials. The evaluation team surveyed consortium members annually through questionnaires and interviews and conducted focus groups in the third, fifth, and sixth years of the evaluation to ascertain perceptions of the effectiveness and accountability of the consortium. Finally, consortium records were collected and analyzed monthly. These records included consortium committee agendas and minutes, monthly reports, and other secondary data. Evaluation reports examined the consortium's development at regular intervals, highlighted issues, identified the consortium's responses to these issues, and proposed recommendations to improve its development. These were shared with co-inquiry teams and consortium committees in the course of the project's implementation.

HOW PAR HELPED THE ALLIANCE
TO BE MORE INCLUSIVE

The project that resulted in the formation of the consortium had been proposed in response to a federal request for proposals (RFP). Although the city government served as the project's fiscal agent, the RFP required that the project itself be a consortium effort reflecting the active involvement of residents and community service providers in all of its phases. As such, local officials and administrators; community residents; and representatives from health, social service, educational, and religious organizations met to begin planning the project. This group became the Administrative Management Group (AMG), the citywide administrative oversight body for the project.

As part of the mandated evaluation component of the project, the staff evaluators began a series of meetings with the AMG to discuss the project and exchange professional ideas about the evaluation process. The staff evaluators initiated preliminary discussions about the use of the PAR process and the philosophy underlying it. Following the initial evaluation meetings, the evaluators and the AMG agreed on an evaluation plan for the project.

One of the first challenges to be addressed at both the citywide and local levels was the identification and recruitment of consortium members. Whereas the initial members of the AMG were identified by the fiscal agent, actions were taken from the beginning to work from within the communities to plan, implement, and monitor the project rather than issue directives from the city level. One of the ways that the AMG identified consortium members was through the implementation of a community survey. The focus of the survey was to develop a group of indigenous community leaders and local service providers to participate in the consortium.

In addition to community surveys conducted to identify potential consortium members, flyers were distributed throughout the neighborhoods, and announcements of consortium meetings were made at church services and other community gatherings. As a result of these initial recruitment efforts, 11 neighborhood councils (NCs) were formed in the project's service delivery area. Their membership included community residents as well as health, social, educational, and religious service providers who worked in the neighborhoods. Citywide service providers and organizations interested in the effort were also recruited through the AMG.

The staff evaluators met with each of the NCs as they were forming to describe the community-based focus of the initiative and the evaluation process. Each council worked to tailor the initiative to its own neighborhood's needs. The general process for this individuation was the identification of assets and barriers within each neighborhood that could be built upon or needed to be addressed in order for the consortium to accomplish its goals. Expanding on the list of assets and barriers, the NCs developed community action plans to achieve specific objectives related to the accomplishment of these goals. Project money was allocated by the AMG to the NCs to implement their action plans, and the neighborhood activities were monitored as part of the evaluation.

The AMG hired staff to coordinate the NCs until the membership was solidified and their own community leaders could be identified. As soon as the councils had selected their leaders, the paid staff assumed a supportive role in the meetings, and the community leaders facilitated the council's discussions and activities.

The AMG responded to the needs of the community leaders by providing training and support in areas identified by them. Sessions included training in community organizing and forums to discuss the challenges of working with community volunteers. Consistent with the PAR methodology, evaluation was an ongoing topic in local council meetings. Cultural competency training was offered to all consortium members. This was deemed necessary because one challenge facing the project was how to successfully integrate the unique range of experiences and access to resources that community residents and service providers brought to the consortium. The leaders worked hard in their training sessions and consortium meetings to ensure that all members had a voice within the consortium.

HOW PAR BUILT TRUST
AMONG THE ALLIANCE'S MEMBERS

Given the history of unfulfilled promises by government-funded groups that had tried to implement programs within the neighborhoods in the past, most NC members were initially skeptical of the sincerity of the consortium's grassroots approach. However, the involvement of representatives from the councils early in the evaluation process was seen as a strength of the project and helped offset some of the skepticism.

As had occurred with the AMG during the assembling phase of the consortium, when the NCs were being established, issues surrounding recruitment and motivation dominated much of their work. To maintain energy and motivation, continuous efforts by the leaders to integrate new members and renew the commitment of the core membership were initiated.

In addition, the members who were service providers struggled with the challenge of balancing their duties to the consortium with their duties to their respective organizations. These conflicting interests occasionally led to battles for control when members put individual or organization concerns above the good of the consortium. In an attempt to manage these competing interests better, the consortium leaders tried to ensure that members clearly understood their roles and how they fit into the context of the overall project. The leaders also served as cheerleaders for the consortium by reminding the members constantly of the importance of the project and commending them for all of their achievements, no matter how modest.

In the weeks following the formation of the NCs and the development of the initial neighborhood action plans, the staff evaluators met with the local leaders to present the PAR strategy. In light of the inclusive nature of the proposed evaluation plan and the community participation sought and nurtured by the AMG, the leaders enthusiastically approved this methodology and agreed to participate in the evaluation process.

Once the commitment of the NCs to work as collaborators in the evaluation was secured, the next step was to form the NC co-inquiry team, which was named the Consortium Leadership Committee (CLC). As a result of earlier discussions, the CLC was established to include two representatives from each NC, and several of the project staff were designated to support the committee. The team immediately began to implement the PAR process.

Data collection included gathering relevant documents from each of the NCs and recording observations of the meetings. The staff evaluators assumed responsibility for synthesizing the data, and team members actively collected the data from the councils and their members. This meant that the team members attended citywide consortium and NC meetings, recorded the content of the discussions, and gathered written materials (i.e., agendas, minutes, memos) used by the groups.

Regular meetings of the CLC were held to discuss and analyze the gathered data. In these meetings, team members exchanged information about how the consortium process was working and which steps or actions might improve the process. Issues that pointed to either strengths or areas needing improvement were identified. Once the issues were identified, co-inquiry team members assisted the consortium members in developing action plans to address these issues.

One issue identified in many of the neighborhoods was the limited number of men who were participating in the project and the NCs. An initiative undertaken to manage this issue was the creation of a new projectwide council that would host activities of particular interest to men and would find relevant ways of connecting them to the project. Although this design for developing neighborhood-specific action plans was a new process for most, the NCs said that they found it useful and in keeping with the spirit of the project's design to gain input from the neighborhood residents and consumers to tailor project activities. The CLC oversaw the implementation of these plans and facilitated the development of a collective understanding of the data and the issues.

Following a similar process, the evaluators created two additional co-inquiry teams representing the administrative and staff levels of the consortium. The focus of these teams was to monitor and improve the effectiveness of the consortium by addressing issues affecting these two constituencies, which often faced matters quite different from each other and from those the community groups were facing. For example, one significant issue for the administrative representatives was a lack of clarity with regard to roles and responsibilities within the consortium. So, the co-inquiry team drafted bylaws for the consortium that, once approved by the project's policy oversight committee, provided structural guidance for the consortium. In response to this concern, the city also added language clarifying roles and responsibilities to its annual subcontracts with organizations receiving funding from the project.

After several back-and-forth moves between the assembling and ordering phases, in response to federal budget reductions and the subsequent restructuring of the program, the consortium was finally able to move more confidently into its ordering phase. The AMG clarified the project's overall mission, and both the AMG and the NCs defined rules and regulations for operating, formalizing internal systems for monitoring budget allocations, and ensuring that information would flow in a timely and efficient manner among all consortium members. As the members considered each of these things in relation to their expectations about the costs and benefits of consortium membership, some left the project. Recruitment and motivation would continue to be prominent issues throughout the performing phase as well.

The AMG tried to further develop the project's governing policies, activities, and programs to accomplish more effectively its overall purpose: the reduction of infant mortality and the improvement of maternal and child health in the 16 neighborhoods. The co-inquiry teams became active participants in monitoring the need for, and effectiveness of, the project's policies and activities.

The performing phase of the consortium's development was characterized by the implementation and monitoring of tasks by the consortium in both the neighborhoods and projectwide. The co-inquiry teams continued data collection and analysis with emphasis on refining the tasks to achieve better outcomes for consumers. Revisions included some restructuring and the hiring of additional staff to support community development activities by creating referral linkages with county-based service providers working with related consumer groups and strengthening ties with the public school system. Project findings and recommendations for improvement were presented at meetings at all levels of the consortium by the project's staff evaluators to solicit broader feedback on issues and enhance implementation of the recommendations.

As the consortium reached the end of its 6-year demonstration phase and prepared to move into a second cycle of federal funding at a substantially reduced amount, the alliance moved into the transforming phase of development. Although the formal collaborative was not disbanding, it was enacting large-scale changes that would fundamentally alter the composition and operations of the project.

Because the core consortium was not dissolving, it continued to implement tasks associated with the performing phase, such as holding committee meetings, delivering services to participants, and sponsoring community events. However, at the same time, the leaders' focus on evaluation shifted. The consortium had engaged in internal monitoring for program improvement through the first 6 years, but evaluation at this stage was motivated by the need to document outcomes and initiate systemic reforms to transition the project out of its demonstration period.

The co-inquiry teams were examining consortium processes and products to document successes, identify aspects of the program that could be eliminated, and plan appropriate changes. In addition, because the subcontract for the consortium evaluation was concluding as well, the co-inquiry teams were preparing to continue their ongoing evaluation efforts without the staff evaluators. This process was facilitated by the fact that, from the outset, the evaluation was team driven and directed. Therefore, team members had learned the skills and developed the trust required to maintain the evaluation efforts without the staff.

REFLECTIONS AND MORE LESSONS LEARNED

In sum, the creation of the co-inquiry teams has served as a normalizing model for the consortium members. Members state that they have found it reassuring and affirming to see that the issues with which they have struggled are shared by others in the larger community, and that they have found the coordinating and facilitating function of the teams helpful. The creation of co-inquiry teams early in the assembling phase ensured that input from the multiple levels of the consortium were represented in the evaluation process. Indeed, regular feedback sessions to continuously analyze the data and plan next steps were an essential feature of the participatory action research design. With each phase of the consortium's development, the co-inquiry teams were required to go through this research cycle at least once—from gathering data to evaluation. Team members have worked collaboratively to improve the process by identifying interpersonal tensions and other potential obstacles, and, together, they devised strategies to minimize these obstacles.

Using the PAR approach had several important benefits. The participation of consortium members in data collection allowed the evaluators to capture information specifically identified as important to the functioning of the consortium and its many councils—information that might have been overlooked in a nonparticipatory process. By participating first in the identification and prioritization of neighborhood issues and then in the development and implementation of action plans to address these issues, the members of the consortium and local councils found it easier to think beyond their individual areas of interest and to be committed to the success of the entire project. And, finally, the assessment of the progress, process, and results of the consortium that took place throughout the evaluation process led to the collection of additional and useful data that might otherwise have been overlooked, thus enabling the project's participants and staff to improve the effectiveness of the initiative.

To summarize, the PAR approach allows for the empowerment of all those involved in the evaluation in at least four important ways. First, it recognizes and works from the strengths and needs of all of the members. Second, it provides members with tools that can be used in managing other difficult or threatening issues that will arise in the future, thereby decreasing their dependence on external "experts." Third, PAR methodology serves to facilitate the identification of new leadership, and nurtures and educates those people in the skills they will need to be effective. And fourth, the very essence of PAR itself can be conducive to building trust both among the alliance members and between the alliance and its environmental linkages.

Whatever the form of the alliance—from affiliation to joint venture or even consolidation—a participatory evaluation can be an integral part of the process. Indeed, as we have seen, it can be a means of clarifying issues, building credibility and trust among the members, focusing them on the larger interests of the alliance, and even pointing the way to creating a more effective alliance.

NOTE

1. An earlier version of these evaluation questions appeared in Bailey and Koney (1995b). The material is reprinted here with permission from ELSEVIER Science.

AFTERWORD

The formation of interorganizational alliances has a long-standing tradition—surely for as long as people have been forming systems by which to address their own needs and the needs of their families and communities. In a more formal sense, organizational studies document a history that runs the length of this century, at least. Social work has been a part of that tradition, demonstrating an understanding of the importance of partnering skills and resources from the early days of the profession, in the interests of best serving those we seek to help. As noted in a 1903 report of the Social Education Committee of the Charity Organization Society, we have "long been organizing interagency collaborations and promoting interagency cooperation" (K. Kendall, 2000, p. 67).

And yet our efforts as a profession in this area have been inconsistent—in education, research, and practice. Commitments to divergent, and sometimes conflicting, goals, as well as struggles to evolve a professional identity in a changing world, have found social work, at times, following other professions' attention to alliances, or ignoring it all together. Still, the essence of our profession *is* a commitment to rally whatever best forces and resources are available to serve those in need effectively.

This fundamental commitment propels us to the cutting edge of leadership for creative thought and action in interorganizational relationships. This book offers one voice of an evolving dialogue, harking back to our early roots as a profession and responding to current imperatives that call us forward into the future. In this regard, as stated at the outset, we invite you, the readers, to engage in this dialogue wholeheartedly. Join us in an ongoing, dynamic partnership of moving the profession and those we serve forward into an exciting future where innovative and fruitful alliances better support us all.

GLOSSARY

Acquisition. A formal strategic alliance model in which one or more organizations cede control of their organizations' board memberships to another organization; sometimes used to emphasize an unequal relationship among organizations in a merger.

Affiliation; Federation. A loosely connected strategic alliance model in which two or more organizations come together to share similar interests; sometimes called a network.

Assembling. The first phase in strategic alliance development when potential partner organizations come together to explore the possibility of forming an alliance.

Association. A minimally formal strategic alliance model in which member organizations relinquish some autonomy to centralize specific organizational functions or tasks.

Coadunation. The most formal strategic alliance process in which organizations unite within an integrated structure to the extent that one or all relinquish their autonomy in favor of a surviving organization.

Coalition. A minimally formal strategic alliance model in which organizations agree to relinquish a minimal amount of organizational autonomy to achieve a political or social change.

Collaboration. A moderately formal strategic alliance process in which organizations work collectively through common strategies, with each relinquishing some degree of autonomy toward the realization of a jointly determined purpose.

Community-based alliance. An interorganizational relationship characterized by an overall identification with a particular locale or issue. Individuals and organizations view themselves as linked, and members from all levels of that community are involved in the combined work.

Consolidation.   A formal strategic alliance model in which two or more organizations are fully dissolved and one newly incorporated organization assumes the assets and liabilities of the dissolved organizations.

Consortium.   A moderately formal strategic alliance model in which organizations that identify with a particular community or interest domain integrate their resources and strategies to accomplish a jointly defined goal within that domain.

Cooperation.   An informal strategic alliance process through which fully autonomous organizational entities share information to support each other's activities.

Coordination.   A minimally formal strategic alliance process in which otherwise autonomous organizations align activities, sponsor particular events, or deliver targeted services in pursuit of compatible goals.

Domain influence.   The focus on increasing power or control as a driving force for HSOs in strategic alliance formation and maintenance.

Due diligence.   A systematic process of assessing an organization's financial, legal, and operational status prior to engaging in a formal strategic alliance.

Environmental linkages.   Relationships that the leaders and members of a strategic alliance collectively form with external individuals and organizations to support the alliance's work.

Environmental validity.   The focus on increasing credibility or enhancing interactions with organizational stakeholders as a driving force for HSOs in the formation and maintenance of strategic alliances.

Federation.   See **Association.**

Formalization.   The extent to which interactions among participating members in an interorganizational relationship are governed by policies, procedures, contracts, or laws.

General partnership.   One way to structure a joint venture in which partners share liability and decision-making powers based on state corporate statutes.

Horizontal network.   A moderately formal network composed of organizations that provide similar services.

Integration.   The extent to which participating members in an interorganizational relationship are linked and thereby interdependent on each other to achieve their goals.

Joint venture.   A moderately formal strategic alliance model in which two or more organizations maintain joint ownership of a legally defined entity to carry out a specific project or deliver certain services; sometimes used broadly to describe the range of collaborative strategic alliance models.

Leadership.   The individuals and/or organizations that formally and informally direct a strategic alliance.

Limited Liability Company.   One way to structure a joint venture that provides a unique set of legal protections and tax ramifications for member organizations based on state corporate statutes.

Limited partnership.   One way to structure a joint venture that provides certain legal protections and puts limits on partners' decision-making powers based on state corporate statutes.

Management service organization.   A network in which organizations centralize management or administrative functions in one organizational entity.

Membership.   The individuals and/or organizations that work with the leaders and collectively comprise a strategic alliance.

Merger.   A formal strategic alliance model in which one or more organizations dissolve, and their assets and liabilities are absorbed by another existing organization.

Network.   A moderately formal strategic alliance model in which organizations create integrated administrative or service delivery systems to increase efficiency or secure managed care service contracts; sometimes used informally to describe an affiliation.

Operational efficiency.   The focus on increasing economies of scale in service delivery or operations as a driving force for HSOs in strategic alliance formation and maintenance.

Ordering.   The second phase of strategic alliance development in which leaders and members define the strategies, structure, and systems of the alliance.

Outcomes.   The measurable attainments achieved as a result of the strategic alliance.

Performing.   The third phase of strategic alliance development during which the leaders and members engage in the tasks necessary to operationalize the alliance.

Preconditions.   The driving forces motivating the formation and maintenance of strategic alliances.

Process.   The way in which the strategic alliance is developed and sustained.

Public-private partnership.   A strategic alliance involving organizations from both the public sector (i.e., government) and the private sector (i.e., nongovernmental organizations).

Purpose.   The shared values, mission, and goals of a strategic alliance.

Resource interdependence.   The focus on maintaining or acquiring resources as a driving force for HSOs in strategic alliance formation and maintenance.

Social responsibility.   The focus on addressing a broad-based community issue or responding to public expectations as a driving force for HSOs in strategic alliance formation and maintenance.

Strategic alliance.   Any of a variety of models of intentional, interorganizational relationships engaged in to benefit the organizational partners and, ultimately, the organizations' consumers.

Strategic enhancement.   The focus on achieving competitive advantage or preserving organizational survival as the driving force for HSOs in strategic alliance formation and maintenance.

Strategies.   The ways or approaches through which a strategic alliance seeks to achieve its purpose.

Structural complexity.   The extent to which an interorganizational relationship is composed of multiple, interrelated parts.

Structure.   The way people and tasks are organized within a strategic alliance to achieve its purpose.

Systems.   The operating ties that define the structure and operations of a strategic alliance.

Tasks.   The specific activities that operationalize the strategies of a strategic alliance.

Transforming.   The fourth phase in strategic alliance development in which alliance leaders and members formally reassess their commitments to the alliance and determine if the alliance will continue, be modified, or end.

Vertical network.   A moderately formal network composed of organizations that offer different and often specialized services.

REFERENCES

Adizes, I. (1979). Organizational passages: Diagnosing and treating life-cycle problems in organizations. *Organizational Dynamics, 8*(1), 3-21.

Alter, C. (1990). An exploratory study of conflict and coordination in interorganizational service delivery systems. *Academy of Management Journal, 33,* 478-502.

Arsenault, J. (1998). *Forging nonprofit alliances: A comprehensive guide to enhancing your mission through joint ventures and partnerships, management service organizations, parent corporations, and mergers.* San Francisco: Jossey-Bass.

Avrunin, W. (1981). What is federation?—A definition for those engaged in making it work. *Journal of Jewish Communal Service, 58,* 209-216.

Bailey, D. (1992a). Organizational change in a public school system: The synergism of two approaches. *Social Work in Education, 14*(2), 71-82.

Bailey, D. (1992b). Using participatory research in community consortia development and evaluation: Lessons from the beginning of a story. *American Sociologist, 23*(4), 71-82.

Bailey, D., & Grochau, K. E. (1993). Aligning leadership needs to the organizational stage of development: Applying management theory to nonprofit organizations. *Administration in Social Work, 17*(1), 23-45.

Bailey, D., & Koney, K. M. (1995a). Community-based consortia: One model for creation and development. *Journal of Community Practice, 2*(1), 21-42.

Bailey, D., & Koney, K. M. (1995b). An integrative framework for the evaluation of community-based consortia. *Evaluation and Program Planning, 18,* 245-252.

Bailey, D., & Koney, K. M. (1996). Interorganizational community-based collaboratives: A strategic response to shape the social work agenda. *Social Work, 41,* 602-611.

Beatrice, D. F. (1990). Inter-agency coordination: A practitioner's guide to a strategy for effective social policy. *Administration in Social Work, 14*(4), 45-59.

Beckhard, R., & Harris, R. T. (1987). *Organizational transitions: Managing complex change* (2nd ed.). Reading, MA: Addison-Wesley.

Bing, L. J. (1938). *Social work in Greater Cleveland: How public and private agencies are serving human needs.* Cleveland, OH: The Welfare Federation of Cleveland.

Black, T. R. (1983). Coalition building: Some suggestions. *Child Welfare, 62,* 263-268.

Boissevain, J. (1974). *Friends of friends: Networks, manipulators and coalitions.* New York: St. Martin's.

Boone, D., & Mannino, F. V. (1965). Cooperative community efforts in mental health. *Public Health Reports, 80,* 189-193.

Chandler, A. D., Jr. (1962). *Strategy and structure: Chapters in the history of American industrial enterprise.* Boston: MIT Press.

Checkoway, B. (1987). Political strategy for social planning. In F. M. Cox, J. L. Erlich, J. Rothman, & J. E. Tropman (Eds.), *Strategies of community organization: Macro practice* (4th ed., pp. 326-342). Itasca, IL: F. E. Peacock.

Cleveland Federation for Charity and Philanthropy. (1913, December). *The social year book: The human problems and resources of Cleveland.* Cleveland, OH: Author.

Cohen, L., Baer, N., & Satterwhite, P. (n.d.). *Developing effective coalitions: An eight step guide.* (Available from Prevention Institute, 1181 Colusa Avenue, Berkeley, CA 94707.)

Croan, G. M., & Lees, J. F. (1979, May). *Building effective coalitions: Some planning considerations.* Washington, DC: U.S. Department of Justice, Law Enforcement Assistance Administration.

Cutlip, S. M. (1965). *Fund raising in the United States: Its role in America's philanthropy.* New Brunswick, NJ: Rutgers University Press.

Dluhy, M. J., with the assistance of Kravitz, S. L. (1990). *Building coalitions in the human services.* Newbury Park, CA: Sage.

Elden, M. (1987). Sharing the research work: Participative research and its role demands. In P. Reason & J. Rowan (Eds.), *Human inquiry: A sourcebook of new paradigms research* (pp. 253-266). New York: Wiley.

Emenhiser, D. L., King, D. W., Joffe, S. A., & Penkert, K. S. (1998). *Networks, mergers, and partnerships in a managed care environment.* Washington, DC: CWLA Press.

Fisher, R., & Karger, H. J. (1997). *Social work and community in a private world: Getting out in public.* New York: Longman.

Flynn, C. C., & Harbin, G. L. (1987). Evaluating interagency coordination efforts using a multidimensional, interactional, developmental paradigm. *Remedial and Special Education, 8*(3), 35-44.

Freire, P. (1970). *Pedagogy of the oppressed.* New York: Continuum.

French, J. R. P., Jr., & Raven, B. (1959). The bases of social power. In D. Cartwright (Ed.), *Studies in social power* (pp. 150-167). Ann Arbor: University of Michigan, Research Center for Group Dynamics, Institute for Social Research.

Gentry, M. E. (1987). Coalition formation and processes. *Social Work With Groups, 10*(3), 39-54.

Glaser, J. S. (1994). *The United Way scandal: An insider's account of what went wrong and why.* New York: Wiley.

Gray, B. (1989). *Collaborating: Finding common ground for multiparty problems.* San Francisco: Jossey-Bass.

Gray, B., & Ariss, S. S. (1985). Politics and strategic change across organizational life cycles. *Academy of Management Review, 10,* 707-723.

Gray, B., & Wood, D. J. (1991). Collaborative alliances: Moving from practice to theory. *Journal of Applied Behavioral Science, 27*(1), 3-22.

Hage, J., & Aiken, M. (1967). Relationship of centralization to other structural properties. *Administrative Science Quarterly, 2*(1), 72-92.

Hasenfeld, Y., & Schmid, H. (1989). The life cycle of human service organizations: An administrative perspective. *Administration in Social Work, 13,* 243-269.

Haynes, K. S., & Mickelson, J. S. (1997). *Affecting change: Social workers in the political arena* (3rd ed.). New York: Longman.

Janis, I. L. (1972). *Victims of groupthink.* Boston: Houghton-Mifflin.

Kagan, S. L. (1991). *United we stand: Collaboration for child care and early education services.* New York: Teachers College Press.

Kahn, S. (1991). *Organizing: A guide for grassroots leaders* (rev. ed.). Silver Spring, MD: NASW Press.

Kanter, R. M., Stein, B. A., & Jick, T. D. (1992). *The challenge of organizational change: How companies experience it and leaders guide it.* New York: Free Press.

Kendall, K. (2000). Social work education: Its origins in Europe. Alexandria, VA: Council on Social Work Education.

Koebel, C. T., Steinberg, R., & Dyck, R. (1998). Public-private partnerships for affordable housing: Definitions and applications in an international perspective. In C. T. Koebel (Ed.), *Shelter and society: Theory, research, and policy for nonprofit housing* (pp. 39-69). Albany: State University of New York Press.

Kohm, A. (1998). Cooperating to survive and thrive: Innovative enterprises among nonprofit organizations. *Nonprofit World, 16*(3), 36-44.

La Piana, D. (1997). *Beyond collaboration: Strategic restructuring of nonprofit organizations.* San Francisco: The James Irvine Foundation and the National Center for Nonprofit Boards.

Lawrence, P. R., & Lorsch, J. W. (1969). *Organization and environment: Managing differentiation and integration.* Homewood, IL: Irwin.

Lewin, K. (1946). Action research and minority problems. *Journal of Social Issues, 2,* 34-46.

Mattessich, P. W., & Monsey, B. R. (1992). *Collaboration: What makes it work: A review of research literature on factors influencing successful collaboration.* St. Paul, MN: Amherst H. Wilder Foundation.

McLaughlin, T. A. (1998). *Nonprofit mergers and alliances: A strategic planning guide.* New York: Wiley.

Melaville, A. I., & Blank, M. J., with Asayesh, G. (1993). *Together we can: A guide for crafting a profamily system of education and human services.* Washington, DC: U. S. Department of Education, Office of Educational Research and Improvement, and U. S. Department of Health and Human Services, Office of the Assistant Secretary for Planning and Evaluation.

Murphy, A. M. (1995, August 1). *Formation of networks, corporate affiliations and joint ventures among mental health and substance abuse treatment organizations* (CMHS Publication No. MC95-43). Rockville, MD: Department of Health and Human Services.

O'Brien, J. E., & Collier, P. J. (1991). Merger problems for human service agencies: A case study. *Administration in Social Work, 15*(3), 19-31.

O'Brien, M. M. (1996, October). *Financing strategies to support comprehensive, community-based services for children and families.* Portland, ME: National Child Welfare Resource Center for Organizational Improvement.

Office of Refugee Resettlement. (1999, February). *Fact sheet* [On-line]. Available: http://www.acf.dhhs.gov/programs/opa/facts/orr.htm (1999, April 27).

Oliver, C. (1990). Determinants of interorganizational relationships: Integration and future directions. *Academy of Management Review, 15,* 241-265.

O'Looney, J. (1994). Modeling collaboration and social services integration: A single state's experience with developmental and non-developmental models. *Administration in Social Work, 18*(1), 61-86.

Parsons, R. J., Jorgensen, J. D., & Hernandez, S. H. (1994). *The integration of social work practice.* Pacific Grove, CA: Brooks/Cole.

Perlmutter, F. D. (1990). *Changing hats: From social work practice to administration.* Silver Spring, MD: NASW Press.

Peterson, N. L. (1991). Interagency collaboration under Part H: The key to comprehensive, multidisciplinary, coordinated infant/toddler intervention services. *Journal of Early Intervention, 15*(1), 89-105.

Reitan, T. (1998). Theories of interorganizational relations in the human services. *Social Service Review, 72,* 285-309.

Romanofsky, P. (Ed.). (1978). Social service organizations. *Greenwood encyclopedia of American institutions* (Vol. 2). Westport, CT: Greenwood.

Roberts-DeGennaro, M. (1986). Factors contributing to coalition maintenance. *Journal of Sociology and Social Welfare, 13,* 248-264.

Roberts-DeGennaro, M. (1987). Patterns of exchange relationships in building a coalition. *Administration in Social Work, 11*(1), 59-67.

Rosenthal, B., & Mizrahi, T. (1994). *Strategic partnerships: How to create and maintain interorganizational collaborations and coalitions.* New York: Education Center for Community Organizing.

Salamon, L. M. (1997). *Holding the center: America's nonprofit sector at a crossroads: A report for the Nathan Cummings Foundation.* New York: Nathan Cummings Foundation.

Schein, E. (1987). *Organizational culture and leadership.* San Francisco: Jossey-Bass.

Schopler, J. H. (1987). Interorganizational groups: Origins, structure, and outcomes. *Academy of Management Review, 12,* 702-713.

Singer, M., & Yankey, J. A. (1991). Organizational metamorphosis: A study of eighteen nonprofit mergers, acquisitions, and consolidations. *Nonprofit Management and Leadership, 1,* 357-369.

Synergos Institute. (1992). *Holding together: Collaborations and partnerships in the real world.* New York: Author.

Tichy, N. M. (1987). Problem cycles in organizations and the management of change. In J. R. Kimberly, R. H. Miles, & Associates (Eds.), *The organizational life cycle: Issues in the creation, transformation, and decline of organizations* (pp. 164-183). San Francisco: Jossey-Bass.

Tuckman, B. W., & Jensen, M. A. C. (1977). Stages of small-group development revisited. *Group & Organization Studies, 2,* 419-427.

Van de Ven, A. H., & Ferry, D. C. (1980). *Measuring and assessing organizations.* New York: Wiley.

Wernet, S., & Jones, S. (1992). Merger and acquisition activity between nonprofit social service organizations: A case study. *Nonprofit and Voluntary Sector Quarterly, 21,* 367-380.

Whetten, D. A. (1981). Interorganizational relations: A review of the field. *Journal of Higher Education, 52*(1), 1-28.

Whyte, W. F. (1991). *Participatory action research.* Newbury Park, CA: Sage.

Winer, M., & Ray, K. (1994). *Collaboration handbook: Creating, sustaining, and enjoying the journey.* St. Paul, MN: Amherst H. Wilder Foundation.

Wolfe, D. M. (1980, August). *On the research participant as co-inquirer.* Paper presented at the annual meeting of the Academy of Management, Detroit.

Yankey, J. A., Koney, K. M., Bailey, D., & Wester, B. (1999). *Strategic alliances: Preconditions, process, and performance.* (Available from the Mandel Center for Nonprofit Organizations, 10900 Euclid Avenue, Cleveland, OH 44106-7167)

Yankey, J. A., Wester, B., & Campbell, D. (1998). Managing mergers and consolidations. In R. L. Edwards, J. A. Yankey, & M. A. Altpeter (Eds.), *Skills for effective management of nonprofit organizations* (pp. 492-503). Washington, DC: NASW Press.

Young, D. R., Bania, N., & Bailey, D. (1996). Structure and accountability: A study of national nonprofit associations. *Nonprofit Management and Leadership, 6,* 347-365.

Zlotnik, J. L. (n.d.). *Social work education and public human services: Developing partnerships.* Alexandria, VA: Council on Social Work Education.

AUTHOR INDEX

SUBJECT INDEX

ABOUT THE AUTHORS

DARLYNE BAILEY, PhD, is Dean and Professor at the Mandel School of Applied Social Sciences at Case Western Reserve University in Cleveland, Ohio. She has a secondary appointment in the Weatherhead School of Management and chairs the governing body of the Mandel Center for Nonprofit Organizations. Dr. Bailey also chairs the Midwest Deans and Directors Alliance of Schools of Social Work. She obtained her MS in psychiatric social work from Columbia University and her PhD in organizational behavior from Case Western Reserve University.

Dr. Bailey's teaching research and numerous publications focus on community-based strategic alliances, workplace diversity, and organizational redesign. Most notable is her work using participatory action research methodology for program evaluation. Additionally, Dr. Bailey has recently completed a book with Drs. Ellen Netting and Felice Perlmutter on the paradoxes of managerial supervision.

KELLY McNALLY KONEY, MSSA, is a nonprofit management consultant with more than 10 years of experience working with human service administrators in the areas of planning and evaluation. In addition, she is a research consultant with the Strategic Alliance Research Initiative at the Mandel Center for Nonprofit Organizations at Case Western Reserve University. Her research and consulting interests include the development and evaluation of interorganizational, community-based alliances and resident involvement in program planning and decision making.

Ms. Koney has co-authored several articles on strategic alliances in the nonprofit sector. She co-teaches a course on interorganizational relations in the master's program at the Mandel School of Applied Social Sciences and conducts workshops on how to form and sustain community partnerships. She received her Master of Science in Social Administration from the Mandel School of Applied Social Sciences at Case Western Reserve University.